My
Analysis
with
FREUD

BY
JOSEPH WORTIS

JASON ARONSON INC.
Northvale, New Jersey
London

THE MASTER WORK SERIES

First softcover edition 1994

Copyright © 1984 by Jason Aronson Inc.

Library of Congress Cataloging-in-Publication Data

Wortis, Joseph, 1906–
    [Fragments of an analysis with Freud]
    My analysis with Freud / by Joseph Wortis.
       p. cm.
    Originally published: Fragments of an analysis with Freud, 5th
English ed. New York : Aronson, 1984.
    Includes index.
    ISBN: 1-56821-394-8
    1. Psychoanalysis. 2. Freud, Sigmund, 1856–1939. I. Title.
    [DNLM: 1. Freud, Sigmund, 1856–1939. 2. Psychoanalysis—history.
3. Psychoanalytic Theory—personal narratives. WM 460 W934f 1984a]
BF173.F85W6 1994
150.19′52—dc20
DNLM/DLC
for Library of Congress   94-34614

Manufactured in the United States of America. Jason Aronson Inc. offers books and cassettes. For information and catalog write to Jason Aronson Inc., 230 Livingston Street, Northvale, New Jersey 07647.

Table of Contents

Foreword

In 1934 Sigmund Freud was 78 years old and Joseph Wortis was 28. Introduced by Havelock Ellis and Adolph Meyer, Wortis met Freud and saw him in regular psychoanalytic sessions for five months (the total fee was $1,600). Wortis had completed his medical training in Vienna a few years earlier, and was pursuing special studies following his psychiatric internship at Bellevue. Freud was burdened by the cancer that was to end his life a few years later, and by the political cancer that was invading central Europe. However he was active professionally with a busy practice, and scientifically having just completed Moses and Monotheism. *Wortis was supported by a fellowship to study sexual psychology and homosexuality, although his interests were far broader than that would suggest. It was only a few months after seeing Wortis that Freud wrote his famous letter to the American mother of a homosexual son. "Homosexuality is assuredly no advantage, but it is nothing to be ashamed of, no vice, no degradation; it cannot be classified as an illness...."[1] Wortis wanted to learn about psychoanalysis, and Freud loved to teach ("I prefer a student ten times more than a neurotic")[2]. Wortis kept careful notes of the sessions, although he never tells us what Freud thought of the notetaking project, or indeed whether Freud even knew about it. This book is largely the result of those notes.*

In a brief 200 pages Wortis provides us with a vivid snapshot, rather than a formal portrait, of Freud. We also get an intriguing glimpse of Wortis himself. This is an important time in Wortis's life; he is about to have his first child ("Freud was very glad to hear my wife was pregnant. 'It is high time,' he said"), and is formulating that special mixture of neurobiology, social behaviorism, and above all rigorous scientific thinking that is the hallmark of his future work. We get a glimpse of a brilliant young man crystallizing the ideas that will persist through his most creative career.

However, the book is by no means an autobiography, and Wortis is careful to keep the focus on Freud and their relationship, not himself. Actually it is about Freud the person, the teacher, perhaps the social critic, rather than Freud the psychoanalyst. Five months of meeting for the purpose of illustrating the method for a student who had no complaint and didn't even plan to become a psychoanalyst may have provided Wortis with a fascinating experience, and it is fascinating to eavesdrop on it now, but it was not really a psychoanalysis even by the standards of 1934. However we do learn a great deal about Freud's thoughts and his clinical "style," often in his own words. ("You have made everything you said up to now so clear it has not interested me...."[3] "That dream is not of much importance."[4] "The analyst does not say all that he thinks, but lets the subject talk until he reaches a point or topic that can be used in the analysis."[5] "All interpretations are tentative... One cannot work from a single dream, one must have a series of them, and fill them into the general scheme.")[6]

Wortis is a difficult "patient." He is frequently late for appointments, always with an excuse, engages the professor in theoretical discussions and argues with him about theories and people. Freud allows himself to get drawn into these arguments, and seems to give up on a therapeutic psychoanalysis very early if indeed he ever thought of conducting one. Diagnostically, today we would probably think in terms of narcissistic personali-

ty. *For Freud, Wortis was a "so-called normal person"
("sogenannten gesunden"), although with an "unwillingness to
accept facts that are unpleasant" that was termed "narcissistic."
Freud interprets the central dynamic of the treatment in the first
month:*

"You wanted to impress me," said Freud.

*"I don't think so," I said. "I was just curious to know how you
approached a problem and tackled it."*

*"But that is not what an analysis is for," said Freud. "You are
not here to get things out of me, wise words and the like; all that
has nothing to do with the analysis."*

*"But it is tempting," I said, "...because you are a great
man..."[7] Wortis goes far to provoke Freud's wise words: "I felt
the best way to coax him to say something was to say the opposite."[8]*

*We can watch the process at another level as well, for Wortis
is a "good" dreamer and he tells us his dreams. On New Year's
eve: "I was driving an auto, but was making many mistakes, and
almost had an accident.... I was driving in Austria," and the
same night "I was in a mountain hotel, among women and men
resembling doctors, and a certain doctor from the eye clinic was
frying eggs.... I knew the doctor too slightly and did not like
him particularly."[9] Freud suggests that the dream has to do with
sex and Wortis's wife (Wortis's first child is born nine months
later!). We might add today that the patient seems to be worried
about his performance on the couch and angry at the doctor
who is challenging him.*

*A few months after Wortis and Freud separate, Adolph
Meyer sees the notes and writes that they are "one of the most
naturally convincing and illuminating documents or memoranda that I could conceive of."[10] Today, almost fifty years later,
one can only agree. The reader must be aware that this was not
a psychoanalysis, and that these are anecdotes that occured during a treatment, rather than an account of the treatment itself.*

Foreword

Yet Wortis is an excellent reporter, Freud a fascinating subject, and this book will be richly rewarding to anyone interested in Freud, or in the history of psychoanalysis and psychiatry.

Robert Michels, M.D.
Chairman, Department of Psychiatry
Cornell Medical Center, New York.

NOTES

1. *Letters of Sigmund Freud* (1980) Selected and edited by Ernst L. Freud. New York: Basic Books, p. 423

2. Wortis, J. (1984) *Fragments of An Analysis with Freud*. New York: Aronson, p. 18

3. Wortis, p. 26

4. Wortis, p. 23

5. Wortis, p. 39

6. Wortis, p. 83

7. Wortis, p. 58

8. Wortis, p. 94

9. Wortis, pp. 125-26

10. Wortis, p. 168

Preface

THIS IS A BOOK *about Sigmund Freud and his theories, and not about me. Freud exerted a deep influence on his generation, and in this country at least an even greater influence on the generation that followed him. This is not the place to do justice to his contributions or to elaborate on their significance. My main purpose is to give a picture of Freud as I saw him, and an account of some of his methods and views. Having had the opportunity as a student in my twenties to meet with him daily over a period of months, and having kept a diary of these meetings, I now feel it is time to spread the record out for general use.*

The record is unique in more than one respect. Not only was it kept accurate and complete, but the circumstances surrounding the experience were unusual. As a young psychiatrist holding a fellowship under the guidance and sponsorship of Havelock Ellis and Adolf Meyer, both of whom maintained a certain critical detachment from the psychoanalytic movement, I entered into a didactic analysis against the advice of Ellis, but with some scepticism of my own. For that reason a large proportion of the discussions with Freud dealt with questions of basic psychiatric theory. Freud permitted me to review his writings as we went along and I was bold or foolish enough to query the theories or formulations that I could not accept or grasp. Meanwhile I kept corresponding with my two aged mentors far away.

I thus found myself in the position of being a young man closely influenced by three very distinguished old men, each of whom held to quite distinctive points of view. It was a situation which was not likely to contribute to any rapid consolidation of opinion and at times I felt badly battered by the pressures and uncertainties. And since the theories had to be demonstrated on my person, involving my delicate sensibilities, my situation was not always a pleasant one.

Under the circumstances I was forced to find some of the answers for myself, and as my sessions with Freud continued I began to acquire at least the germs of some convictions. In this analytic relationship the subject, myself, thus managed to maintain the unusual posture of a somewhat wavering and conflicted but nonetheless obdurate independence.

I have no intention of perpetuating the discussion on the material of my own person. If I am to be dissected, I would prefer on general humane principles to have it done as a post-mortem. I also have no wish to achieve distinction by posing naked in the street. I have therefore bowdlerized this account without, I am sure, distorting it. I have spared the sensibilities of a few people named in my notes, including muself, by omitting anything of an unduly compromising or embarrassing character. The deletions are however very few and without effect on the essential accuracy of the story. Our conversations were all in German, but I kept my notes in English, with frequent inclusion of the German words and phrases that Freud used. All the quotations are exactly as they stand in my notes, usually written down immediately after each session, in a nearby coffeehouse, on the 4x6-inch cards I always carried with me. The impulse to keep a record of our talks arose quite naturally out of the realization that my period of contact with Freud would be limited, and I wanted to reconsider the experience at leisure. Havelock Ellis, who read all the original notes, wrote, "they do not reveal anything about you." Nevertheless I am sure they will

PREFACE

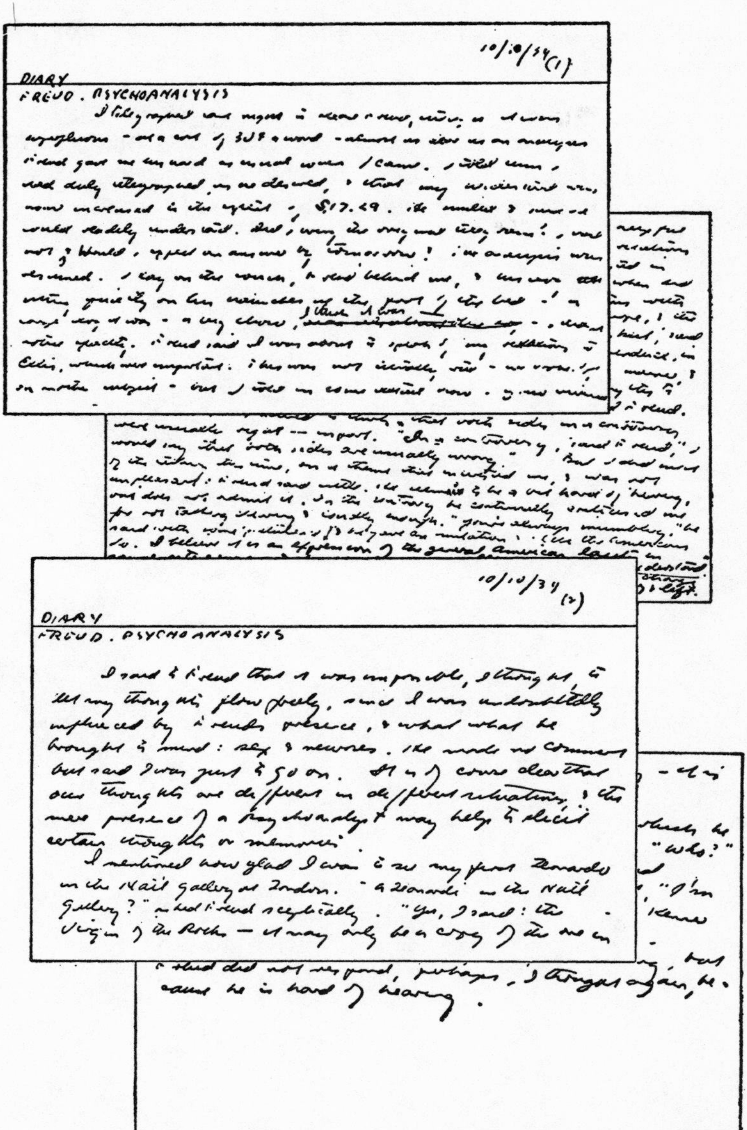
10/10/34 (1)
DIARY
FREUD . PSYCHOANALYSIS
10/10/34 (2)
DIARY
FREUD . PSYCHOANALYSIS
I said to Freud that it was impossible, I thought, to let my thoughts flow freely, since I was undoubtedly influenced by Freud's presence, & what what he brought to mind: sex & neuroses. He made no comment but said I was just to go on. It is of course clear that our thoughts are different in different situations, & the mere presence of a psychoanalyst may help to elicit certain thoughts or memories.
I mentioned how glad I was to see my first Leonardo in the Natl Gallery at London. "A Leonardo in the Natl Gallery?" asked Freud sceptically. "Yes, I said: the Virgin of the Rocks — it may only be a copy of the one in
Freud did not respond, perhaps, I thought again, because he is hard of hearing.

supply plentiful material for fanciful elaboration for those who like that sort of thing.

Thanks are due to the American Journal of Psychiatry *and to the* American Journal of Orthopsychiatry *for permission to reprint material previously published in those journals.*

My
Analysis
with
FREUD

THE CIRCUMSTANCES

THE circumstances leading to my contacts with Freud were these. In 1927 during my first trip abroad, at the age of twenty, I had the good fortune of meeting Havelock Ellis, a literary and scientific hero of my college days, and we maintained a friendly correspondence throughout the succeeding years of my medical studies abroad. Upon the completion of these studies, while I was serving an interneship at Bellevue Psychiatric Hospital in 1933, Dr. Paul Schilder, who was then Research Professor at the hospital, surprised me one day with the information that Dr. Adolf Meyer of Johns Hopkins Hospital, the leading American psychiatrist of his time, had been making inquiries about me. Before I could begin to wonder, an explanatory letter came from Havelock Ellis:

30 *October,* 1933
24, Holmdene Ave.
Herne Hill
London, S.E. 24

DEAR WORTIS:

Pleased to have your interesting letter and all the instructive remarks about your work at the Hospital.

But today there is specially one matter I want to bring

before you—a point that came to me in the early morning in bed yesterday (my usual time for receiving divine inspirations!). There is a very large sum of money in the good hands of an American friend of mine (and Françoise's) which is, in some as yet undetermined way, to be devoted to the scientific study of homosexuality, with the full study and following up of cases, etc. with the view of illuminating the subject and of promoting a rational and humane attitude towards it. (The holder of the money, I should add, is not personally a sexual invert.) The idea in mind so far has been of a legacy to found a chair at some university or medical school. I am more in favour of selecting a suitable person for the post and enabling him to go ahead as soon as possible (as my friend Mrs. D—— of Chicago has done with such fine results), and my recommendations are likely to be influential in making a decision. It seems to me that you would be peculiarly suitable for this work, and while it would take up a large part of your time, perhaps for life, you would be able to make conditions leaving you free for other neurological etc. work. If I hear that you are willing to consider the matter, I will give you more precise details. So far as I can see, there would be nothing of an undesirable character about the scheme. . . .

With affectionate greetings in which Françoise joins,

HAVELOCK ELLIS

The offer was not only a welcome professional opportunity but brought heartening evidence of confidence from this distinguished source, and I answered at once. At the same time I had no wish at that point to become a sexologist. It seemed to me that there was no longer any need for a revival of the brave pioneering efforts of Ellis of a half century ago. Sex seemed to have found its appropriate acceptance in the world of scientific interest and was indeed beginning to be over-emphasized in some quarters. I also had some doubts and misgivings about a project that might be intended to involve special pleading on behalf of homosexuals. I therefore replied that since I stood at the beginning of my psychiatric training, I would be glad to accept a fellowship of the sort described if it allowed me to pursue my general psychiatric training, with a view to later turning my interest to special studies in the field of sex.

Ellis replied as follows:

16 January, 1934
24 Holmdene Avenue
S.E. 24

DEAR WORTIS:

Pleased to have your letter and our thanks for your New Year's Card!

All your plans and resolutions for the future seem excellent. Long ago I remember my early friend Percival Chubb (now living somewhere in New York, I think) saying that nowadays we must know a little of everything and everything of something. It has always seemed to me sound doctrine, though since then every "something" has become so complex that it is difficult to know everything of it.

I am writing at once to say—though now you may know all about it—that the scheme I wrote to you about is developing. Adolf Meyer of Johns Hopkins, whose advice was asked, has been to Bellevue to make inquiries about you. I have just seen a letter from him in which he says that he hears there from two informants that you are "very unusually talented," and he adds "evidently an interesting person." So it is all

3

right so far, and any farther step rests with you. I believe
you are to hear more this week. . . .

No more now. Françoise joins in affectionate greetings.

HAVELOCK ELLIS

About the same time the following letter came from Dr.
Meyer:

THE JOHNS HOPKINS HOSPITAL

Baltimore, Md.

January 19, 1934

Dr. Joseph Wortis
Bellevue Hospital
New York City
DEAR DOCTOR WORTIS:

I have been asked to talk with you about the possibility of
your undertaking a study of human sex-problems, particularly
with regard to homosexuality, a matter concerning which you
probably have heard from Havelock Ellis. The donor feels
ready to begin with an annual stipend, under the direction of
the Sex Research Committee of the National Research Coun-
cil. In order to protect the enterprise against undesirable pub-
licity the incumbent would be expected to be attached to a
dependable hospital or organization in contact with investiga-
tors in friendly fields. The question arises whether you would
be interested in such a field and whether you would care to
discuss the problem and proposition with me. If your reaction
is one of interest in the proposition I should be glad to hear
what you think of the possibilities and to make contact with
you here or in New York. It might be wise to treat the mat-

4

ter confidentially so as to avoid undesirable curiosity. I should like to have you spend a day with us at the Phipps Clinic (forenoon of some Monday or Wednesday if practicable) if it seems desirable. May I hear from you?

Most sincerely yours,

ADOLF MEYER

Soon afterwards the matter was settled, and I made the following practical proposals to Dr. Meyer:

March 14, 1934

DEAR DR. MEYER:

I have been thinking of plans for the preparation and continuation of the work I have been asked to do, and feel that the main thing just now is to acquaint myself a little better with the literature, and look around and find out what is being done. For the actual technical preparations, there are various possibilities. . . .

Mr. B—— and I talked the matter over and agreed that I would start as soon as possible, and to that end I shall leave in a month or two for London, where I would have the advantage of close association with Ellis, whose knowledge of the literature is certainly extensive. After a few months I could then either return to America or stay in Europe for a while, if it seems advisable, for more clinical or laboratory experience. Though I am myself sceptical of the dogmas and claims of the psychoanalysts, don't you think it would be worth-while to learn something of the subject at first hand? It may be that it could be arranged. I think that it is of first importance too to acquire the *techniques* I may need later,

5

since the book-learning and clinical experience will come easier then. I mean some training in physiology, in biochemical endocrinology and in histo-pathology, as well as in psychoanalysis (or something similar). . . .

Sincerely yours,
JOSEPH WORTIS

Armed with a letter of introduction from Dr. Meyer, my wife and I went on to London where for a period of months I joined in rounds and visited the clinics of Wilson, Collier and Holmes at the Neurological Hospital on Queens Square, and attended clinics at the Maudsley Psychiatric Hospital where Drs. Mapother and Lewis were then active. In addition I began to undertake special reading at the British Museum, where I would meet briefly with Ellis from time to time, and I called upon various scientists in London for discussions and suggestions on my projected work. At one such meeting at London University J. B. S. Haldane told me: "The essence of the sex problem is very simple: too many people think sex behavior is merely the expression of an unconditioned instinct, when it is really the product of conditioning." Later on I had frequent occasion to remember the basic significance of his statement.

At the end of the summer we moved on to Vienna, where I at once wrote to Freud. It was not my first attempt to meet with him. Two years before, after a prolonged residence in Vienna, I had written a note to him, telling him how much helpful stimulus I had from his books and how much I would have liked to meet him before I left, but added that I did not think it right for a student to presume upon the time of so busy a man. He had answered (in German):

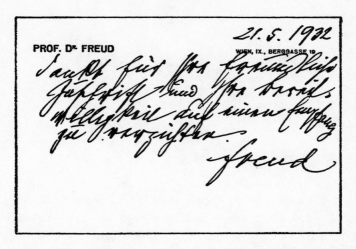

May 21, 1932

PROF. Dr. FREUD
  Thanks you for the friendly note, and for your willingness
to forego a visit.

FREUD

  But this time, under different circumstances, his response
was different.

FIRST MEETINGS

My first meeting with Freud was early in September, 1934, about a week after my arrival in Vienna. I had written to him, told him of my work and references, and had asked for a meeting. There was a telephone message soon after, asking me to come at five o'clock on a Monday, I believe. I confirmed this by phone, and arrived duly just before five at his suburban flat in Grinzing (47 Strassergasse) not far from where I used to live in Himmelstrasse. Freud occupied the lower floor of an undistinguished little apartment house, set back from the road behind an iron fence, with a rather large garden in the rear. A white-haired lady was seated at a table beneath a tree, engaged in knitting—perhaps the Frau Professor, I reflected. Inside, the servant girl told me I was just a few minutes too early. The Herr Professor is always *sehr pünktlich*—very punctual—in everything he does, she confided to me. Would I care to sit in the garden a while? I walked about a bit and returned again and waited.

At five o'clock a youngish lady with a slight squint, apparently an American, came from the professor's study, put on her hat, and left. I entered the room, the professor slipped in from the veranda, offered me his hand, and asked me to sit down. He was short of stature, slight of build, and looked intensely pale and serious. His manner was direct and to the point, and he wasted no time on ceremony. It fell upon me to explain my presence. I told him that I was the recipient of a fellowship which was at first intended for work in the field of sex psychology, that the donors of the fellowship were especially interested in the problem of homosexuality, but that I had insisted that I first prepare myself in the general field of psychiatry before turning to special studies. I was therefore a student and a beginner in the field of psychiatry. Since this work led to an interest in psychoanalysis and in him, I would be grateful for any help he could give me. *"Sie wollen also Psychoanalyse lernen,"* he concluded, with more precision than I had ventured to use. The only way to learn analysis, he went on, is to be psychoanalyzed oneself. The question, in effect, is: where could I be analyzed? That would depend on my means: there are all grades of analysts at different prices. There were no free scholarships for Americans. I told him what my means were and he made a simple calculation: the cheapest analysis would cost so much. He could, if I wished, consult with his daughter and send me some names. He would of course be interested in teaching me himself since I was preparing to be a research worker, but he suspected that his fees would be too high. If my supporters would agree to pay his fees, it could be arranged. He would wait to hear from me.

During the short interview, Freud sat opposite me with a little table between us, facing me directly. Sometimes he bent sideways and leaned on his desk, looking keen and mousy. His speech was low and muffled and the metal appliance in his mouth (which he had worn since his operation) seemed to cause him much annoyance. His German was precise and deliberate, and he spoke his syllables and words with emphasis.

9

He made no bones about asking me a number of questions about myself: my age, my experience, was I neurotic, was I sexually abnormal, was my wife with me now? If I was no *schwerer Neurotiker*—no severe neurotic—an analysis would not be a matter of more than a year, but then *"werden Sie natürlich sehr viel lernen"*—I would naturally learn a lot. Our meeting was concluded when our business ended, all in a matter of fifteen minutes or so. I rose and shook hands again, added a few remarks about Ellis, said there was some news this summer that Freud was in poor health and Ellis was concerned. "All such reports are false," he said. He accompanied me to the door and I left.

Ellis had already offered to write to Freud, but Freud had evidently not yet heard from him.

> *September 7, 1934*
> Haslemere
> Wivelsfield Green
> Haywards Heath, Sussex

DEAR JOSEPH:

I hope you are safely arrived and pleasantly situated in Vienna. . . . How about Freud? If you hear that he is at home and in tolerable health (the last report I heard was unfavorable) I could, if you like, write to him, and back up your request for a meeting. . . .

> Yours ever,
> HAVELOCK ELLIS

Ellis in previous correspondence and in conversation with me had repeatedly indicated that he had grown sceptical of psychoanalysis; he hoped I would not accept its theories and saw no need for me to undertake a didactic analysis. Soon after my fellowship had started he wrote to me (in March 1934), "I agree that endocrinology and mental analysis are the foundations of this and all similar work (I would not myself say Freudian analysis; it is surely better, like Freud himself, to develop a technique of your own). . . ."

At about this time another letter came from Ellis urging me to drop the idea of a personal didactic analysis:

> *September 14, 1934*
> Haslemere

DEAR JOSEPH:

Thank you for your most interesting letter.

About Freud, I am glad to have your detailed account. I had not yet written to him because (as I wrote you) I was waiting to hear some report from you about his present health, etc. I shall write to him now. About being psychoanalysed, my own feeling most decidedly is that it would be better to follow his *example* than his precept. *He* did not begin by being psychoanalysed (never was!) or attaching himself to any sect or school, but went about freely, studying the work of others, and retaining always his own independence. If he had himself followed the advice he gives you, he would have attached himself to Charcot with whom he was working, and become his disciple, like Gilles de la Tourette, an able man and now forgotten. If you are psychoanalysed you either become a Freudian or you don't. If you don't, you remain pretty much where you are now; if you do—you are done for!—unless you break away, like Jung or Adler or Rank (and he has done it too late). To every great leader one may apply the saying of Nietzsche about Jesus:—There has been only one Christian and he died on the cross. There has been only one Freudian! Mr. B—— would like you to be associated with Freud, I know, but that could anyhow be settled.

Good to hear you are already working along useful lines. . . .

Sad about Vienna. I cherish my ancient memories.

Françoise joins in affectionate greetings,

HAVELOCK ELLIS

I shared some of Ellis's scepticism, but had a warmer feeling towards analysis, had read Freud with fascination and was very eager to meet and work with him. Having the chance at last offered to me I did not want to give it up. I at once wrote to Adolf Meyer and to the sponsors of my fellowship, reporting on my meeting with Freud and indicating that I would like to follow his suggestion and undertake a didactic analysis under him; I wrote similarly to Ellis. Soon afterwards Ellis answered, letting me know he had been in touch with Freud and enclosing a typewritten transcript, in German, of Freud's reply to him:

October 4, 1934
24 Holmdene Avenue
London S.E. 24

DEAR JOSEPH:

I have your interesting letter and I gather there is to be analysis under Freud for as long as what money —— sets apart for this purpose allows. —— wrote to me on this point, and I replied (last week) that (as I had already said to you)

I did not myself consider analysis necessary for your work.

But association with Freud for a time will no doubt be valuable. I quite agree that with one of his pupils it would not be worth-while. But there is no question that Freud is a master. I have lately had a letter from him in reply to mine; his ancient script never was very clear to me, so I asked a German girl to copy it. I enclose her version in case you care to see it. Please return it, and no need to mention to Freud that I sent it, though you would perhaps thank him on my behalf for his letter and convey my best greetings. I also have always understood that Freud analysed himself (a simple and economical method!) chiefly by investigating his dreams. . . .

Yours ever,

HAVELOCK ELLIS

The enclosed letter from Freud to Ellis follows in translation:

(end of September, 1934)

DEAR MR. ELLIS:

I was very glad to see your handwriting again and hope you are well. I would wish, better than I.

Dr. Wortis visited me. The knowledge of psychoanalysis which he desires can be acquired in one way, namely by submitting oneself to an analysis. He was willing to do this and regarded it as important to undertake it under me. To me a talented pupil is naturally preferable to a patient. I would be glad to take him on, provided a certain condition is met, and provided I remain well enough to work. The condition concerns the honorarium. I am unfortunately not so successful that I can disregard the matter of making a living, but must sell my few hours of work dearly. If he reports that he cannot come to me I will recommend him to some outstanding pupil of mine. Preferably to my own daughter whom I, and not only I, value as a representative of psychoanalysis. I saw your picture recently in the first issue of an Indian journal (*Marriage Hygiene*).

With cordial regards
yours,
FREUD

Adolf Meyer supported my wish to undergo analysis with Freud and wrote to me later:

October 25, 1934
The Johns Hopkins Hospital
Baltimore, Maryland

DEAR DR. WORTIS,

. . . The main item of your letter is of course your active contact with Freud. You made the right choice, and I made that clear to —— encouraging them to give you the necessary support as far as they could go. . . .

Freud interested me from his debut in the literature and while I felt from the beginning of my medical work keen on the inclusion of all of human nature in the scientific reality and objective world even just as I found it, the systematic organization he gave to it all was and is always stimulating and like a fabric of true art and life. I saw and heard him at Worcester in 1909 and called on him in 1923 and regret that the personal contacts could not have been more frequent and closer. I hope you will be a live link to whom I may turn when

you get back to these shores. To cover such a life-work with
the author while you allow yourself to vibrate true to yourself
and to the atmosphere must be a great satisfaction. . . .

Sincerely yours,
ADOLF MEYER

Freud's next note to me—written in English—reads:

September 29, 1934
Vienna

DEAR MR. WORTIS:

Will you call on me Monday October first half past three
exactly? I will have half an hour to discuss your situation
with you.

Sincerely yours,
FREUD

This time I kept Freud waiting, for I came a minute late,
and noticed him standing at the window looking out to the

gate when I passed through. The American woman with the squint was again in the hall when I came in, and she gave me a friendly smile as I passed by.

Freud waved me to a chair, and I again talked first. I showed him the cablegram I had received offering $1600 for a period of analysis, and Freud did some simple reckoning out loud: the money would keep me in analysis under him for four months. He considered it would be worth while. Since I was not a neurotic, but a student, it was no great matter whether the analysis was complete or not. I could at least learn a great deal; *"und dann werden Sie Lust bekommen es fortzusetzen,"* he added—I would then want to continue. He said he could not agree to use this limited sum of money to give me mere informal theoretical instruction, such as Ellis suggested and I desired. An alternative was to be analyzed by, say, his daughter, *"die eine sehr gute Analytikerin ist"*—a very good analyst—at much less cost, for a longer time. I replied it was simply a question of Freud or nothing for the present; so far as I was concerned I was ready to start, on the understanding that these four months would be reasonably adequate. Freud thought this possible, but it would depend on my *Aufnahmefähigkeit* or receptive capacity, and my *Vorrat* or supply of neurotic material, which after all every civilized person has—*"schliesslich jeder Kulturmensch hat."* I accepted the proposal.

"I ought perhaps to say at the outset," I told Freud, "that I am acting against Ellis's advice." And I read the passage from Ellis's letter, telling me to follow Freud's *example* rather than his *precept*, and go my own independent way. Freud listened with interest and said, "Ellis, in a fundamental sense, has rejected psychoanalysis." I was inclined to deny this, and said he seemed quite sympathetic in many ways, especially toward Freud personally. "I know," said Freud. "Ellis is one of the friendliest persons I know. A man can only accept so and so much of psychoanalysis," he added. "Pfister, author of *Love-life of Children*, for example, could only go to a certain limit because after all he was a minister."

I rather resented the implication that psychoanalysis stood clear and perfect, like divine revelation, and only those could share its secrets who enjoyed grace. "It may very well be that at the end I will reject analysis too," I said, "and I may as well say at the outset that the implication that something is wrong with me for that reason is not very agreeable."

"But it isn't likely that you can form an independent judgment yet," Freud replied. "You are so young."

"Still," I said, "we all have different experiences, and I may some time see something that you have overlooked."

He admitted this hypothetical possibility and we discussed the point for a while. I meant to indicate how unfair the attitude of psychoanalysis to its critics can be. Freud had once written in some essay that those who haven't been analyzed have no right to criticize, and those who are analyzed and then criticize do so because some special sensibilities were stirred.

"I shouldn't like that to be said of me," I said.

"It could be," said Freud, and he then added, whether in regard to himself or me, I don't know, "It is perfectly natural for a person to defend his own opinions."

It was true that he was never analyzed himself: there was nobody there to analyze him. "But I discovered analysis," he said. "That is enough to excuse me. (*Ich habe doch die Psychoanalyse entdeckt. Das kann man mir doch verzeihen.*)" For the rest, he could interpret his own dreams and recollections. I need have no fear, he went on, that I would lose my independence; and that, he added, is a lesson: when I come to analyze others I will discover that my patients will have exactly the same feeling. *"Wir werden sehn.*—We shall see," he repeated. In a week or ten days we would start.

"I prefer a student ten times more than a neurotic," he concluded with a disparaging gesture and a laugh. He rose and gave me his hand, held stiffly, and bent in strangely at the wrist; whether this was a surgical contracture or a mannerism, I did not know. I left.

THE ANALYSIS

Freud wrote me to come at 6 p.m on October 9, 1934 and to confirm the appointment by telephone. I did, but sent a note saying the actual confirmation of the arrangements would have to come from the sponsors of the fellowship, who were to supply the money, though their cablegram indicated there ought to be no trouble on that score. If, for any unseen reason, they changed their minds, Freud would be paid for his services to date. When I arrived, Freud had me sit down and made it clear that he was displeased with this uncertainty: I either agree or disagree to start, and he was unwilling to start before the financial matter was settled. I said that was only a matter of a few days, until my last week's letter arrived in the U.S.A., and nothing would be gained by sending an additional short cablegram, which would not explain the situation. I did not feel it was worth this long discussion; I had no secret plans, and felt there would be no difficulty at all.

"But," said Freud with a characteristic turn of phrase, "the fact remains that you wrote this letter. You didn't want to take the responsibility on yourself, you wanted to share it with me." He finally consented to start anyway, and I was to settle this other business as soon as possible by cabling for a definite commitment.

Freud then made this preliminary statement: an analysis requires an hour a day, five days a week, and starts with a fourteen day trial period, during which both doctor and patient decide whether they care to go on. Thereafter the assumption is that the analysis will continue, though there is nothing really binding.

I was directed to a couch. Freud sat behind me and commenced a little lecture on the ensuing procedure, talking in true lecture style, deliberately and lucidly, while I followed with a periodic *"Ja–Ja."* Our conversation was in German from the outset and remained so to the end.

Freud spoke of the importance of the couch arrangement to assure relaxation and freedom from restraint in the patient. "Besides," he added, "I don't like to have people stare me in the face." He then went on to speak of the fundamental condition for an analysis: absolute honesty—I was to tell literally everything that went through my head: whether important, unimportant, painful, irrelevant, absurd, or insulting. He for his part would guarantee absolute privacy, regardless of what I revealed: murder, theft, treachery or the like. The analyst however is permitted to use the material he thus gathers for scientific ends *für die Analyse,* but must in such cases conceal or disguise anything that would reveal the identity of the patient. It is assumed that the analyst will answer to his own conscience about the uses to which he puts his knowledge. "And," he added, "it is an assumption that every man is honest, until proven otherwise." He then asked me what I knew of analysis, and I told him of my knowledge, which was not very full, something of my general education, and incidentally some details of my history. He found it most convenient, then, he said, to assume I knew nothing, though I was not to take offense, since it was a mere matter of convenience. I remember saying I was first attracted to Freud through Max Eastman's book, *The Sense of Humor.* "A bad book!" said Freud. "And now," he went on, "you can start and say what you like."

I started with the least pleasant of my thoughts. I said the nearest I came to ever having a neurosis was last year when I began to work in a psychiatric hospital, but that I since got over it.

"Without help?" said Freud skeptically. "Only my own help apparently," I said. "At least, I felt distressed then but felt perfectly all right lately." After studying abroad so many years, I felt lost in the big new hospital, was out of touch with things and out of contact with all my old and dearest friends. I found it difficult to slip into the unaccustomed routines of hospital duties, future prospects did not appear bright, and I tended to be discouraged. I found it hard to apply myself to study and began to deprecate my intellectual prowess. All my little failures, real or imaginary, became associated with this sort of harsh self-criticism. Minor physical complaints seemed too important to me and I exaggerated their significance. However, I said, I knew enough of psychoanalysis to realize it was silly and useless to submerge such thoughts, and I made no bones about talking freely of them when there was occasion, most of all to my wife. Fortunately, at this very same time I got the offer of this new work which gave me a wonderful amount of independence, splendid opportunities, and a change of scene. I soon felt very well again and was not troubled by those thoughts. I wanted to go on to say that my interest in hypochondriasis took a scientific turn and seemed to dissolve as I convinced myself that its basis lay in a certain depressive emotional tone, associated with certain bodily sensations, brought on by my situation, experiences, and accompanying tensions at the time. But I was pulled short in the middle, at the end of the hour, to continue next day.

Freud said at the outset that psychoanalysis demands a degree of honesty which is unusual, and even impossible *in der bürgerlichen Gesellschaft* (in bourgeois society); but I on the contrary had never thought that I had to practice any great degree of concealment or dishonesty in the society in which I moved, least of all with my good friends. It brought to mind the question of whether Freud's theories of repression were not limited in their application to the kind of society in which he still seemed to live. I became curious to know whether the kind of life I had lived was not unusual among his analytic subjects. It seemed at any rate fairly typical for my own social group and generation.

For the rest, my first hour proved disturbing for two main reasons: first, because it threatened to revive unpleasant introspective thoughts which led me nowhere and hampered my free activity—and indeed, it was not easy to concentrate on microscopic neurological work and other studies when all my most delicate feelings were being stirred; and second, because there was the unpleasant prospect of developing what Freud called *Widerstand*, or resistance, against him, my present lord and master; who sat in quiet judgment while I talked, like a stern Old Testament Jehovah, and who seemed to take no special pains to act with hospitality or reassurance, but had instead needlessly disturbed our friendly association by what seemed to me to be an over-emphasis on money matters.

October 10, 1934

I cabled last night to please Freud, though it was superfluous, at a cost of thirty cents a word—almost as dear as an analysis. Freud gave me his hand as usual when I came. I told him I had duly telegraphed, as he desired, and that my *Widerstand*, or resistance, was now increased to the extent of seventeen Austrian schillings, twenty-nine groschen. He smiled and said he could readily understand. Did I bring the original telegram? I had not. Would I expect an answer by tomorrow? . . . The analysis was resumed.

I lay on the couch, Freud behind me, his dog sitting quietly on his haunches at the foot of the bed . . . a large dog . . . a big chow I thought it was. . . . I didn't notice exactly. Freud began by saying that I was about to speak of my relations to Ellis, which were important. This was not literally true—we broke off on another subject, but I told in some detail how I grew interested in Ellis, what I thought of him, and how encouraging and helpful he had been. I then went on to give some history of my earlier relationship to my wife, and some more about myself. Freud seemed interested in Ellis, asked occasional questions about him: was he a doctor? when did I first actually meet him?, etc. When I spoke of my adolescent friendship with my wife, described my uncertainty about leaving her when I first came to study in Europe, and the resulting confusion, Freud commented, "In jeder Beziehung liegt eine Abhängigkeit, selbst mit einem Hund. (There is an element of dependence in every relationship, even with a dog.)"

Speaking of Ellis's manner and his friendliness in discussion, I said he never went to great lengths to defend his own views.

"*Er ist nicht rechthaberisch* (he is not self-righteous)," said Freud.

I said Ellis was inclined to think that both sides in a controversy were usually right, in part.

"In a controversy," said Freud, "I would say that both sides are usually wrong."

But I did more of the talking this time on a theme that interested me and was not unpleasant. Freud said little. He seemed to be a bit hard of hearing, but did not admit it. On the contrary he continually criticized me for not talking clearly and loudly enough.

"You're always mumbling," he said with some petulance, and he gave a mumbling imitation, "like the Americans do. I believe it is an expression of the general American laxity in social intercourse, and it is sometimes used as *Widerstand*."

I said I didn't think that applied to my case; it wasn't easy to change years of habit on notice, but I would do my best.

I said to Freud that it was impossible, I thought, to let my thoughts flow freely, since I was undoubtedly influenced by Freud's presence, and what he brought to mind: sex and neuroses. He made no comment but said I was just to go on. It seemed obvious to me that one's thoughts were bound to be different in different situations, and that the mere presence of a psychoanalyst tended to elicit certain thoughts or memories.

I remarked how glad I was to see my first Leonardo in the National Gallery at London.

"A Leonardo in the National Gallery?" asked Freud sceptically.

"Yes," I said: " 'The Virgin of the Rocks.' It may only be a copy of the one in the Louvre . . . or the Louvre may have the copy. . . . It is hard to say and experts disagree."

I mentioned a note Ellis wrote, in which he spoke of his liking for the composer Dukas.

"Who?" asked Freud.

"Dukas," I repeated, and told Freud something about him.

"I don't know," said Freud, *"Ich bin kein grosser Kenner der Musik.* (I'm no great connoisseur of music.)"

I stopped at 7 P.M. and rose to leave, saying, "Goodbye, Herr Professor," but Freud did not respond, perhaps, I thought again, because he was a little hard of hearing.

October 11, 1934

Today's hour was uneventful and rather informal, with perhaps a friendlier atmosphere. I made some comment on one or two books that were on the table; Freud directed me to the couch, and asked me to go on. There was a little confusion at first, because I didn't quite know what to say.

"Say what you're thinking of," said Freud.

"I'm thinking of what to say," said I.

Since this didn't seem likely to get us anywhere, I launched into what turned out to be a lecture on the fundamentals of psychology, a subject which interested me greatly, on which I spoke with vehemence, gesticulating and swinging my arms, and talking in a loud deliberate voice to please Freud. Freud listened with apparent interest, and made occasional remarks. When I attempted to define a neurosis as a maladaptation between an individual and his environment, and said one could prevent neuroses by changing the environment, Freud did not disagree but said that was not a doctor's task.

"For me at least," I said, "I see nothing to hinder me from engaging in work of that kind too." I also said that

25

physical health was an important factor to consider, and that a person in sound health in a friendly environment was not likely to develop a neurosis. A lively pace of productive activity seemed important too: a person on a bicycle proceeding with energy at high speed is not likely to be upset by a stone, but if he travels slowly, a gust of wind will upset him. Individual intrapsychic factors, I felt, were often exaggerated.

"It is not so simple," said Freud.

For the rest, I proceeded to give an account of my vicissitudes in love and life. Freud made friendly and sympathetic remarks here and there, seemed to think I was well-trained in honesty, and said it was *"eine gute Vorbereitung für die Analyse* (a good preparation for analysis)." I said I was not overmuch interested in myself, and felt better when I simply went about my work.

"That is of interest, too," said Freud. "You have made everything you said up to now so clear it has not interested me either."

I did not quite understand what he meant, but went on to the end of the hour, then shook hands twice and left.

October 12, 1934

An uneventful hour. Freud began by saying I ought to bring up more of my problems. I said I had no very serious personal ones. The discouragement and moodiness that I felt last year had slowly disappeared: psychoanalysis had evoked the memory and perhaps it was worth emphasis. Those feelings no longer bothered me, but I would recall them as a sort of symbol of that period, or as something in the background of my thoughts.

I mentioned that I had once spent a summer working for

a schizophrenic relative who was developing delusional ideas that the family was beginning to worry about.

"How old were you then?" Freud asked.

"Sixteen," I said. "It didn't affect me much at the time, but later on when I was told of the importance of heredity, it did concern me for a little while."

"But the heredity is recessive," said Freud.

I said I also exploited this interest for scientific ends, studied the subject, and came to independent conclusions. I did not even believe it was recessive in heredity, and the statistical studies were unconvincing since I could not see how a diagnosis could be made fifty years or two generations back, before the term "schizophrenic" was even known. Anyway, I said, I proposed to talk this hour of all the various painful thoughts I had ever had—which I did: various conscience-pangs, self-reproaches and anxieties, though none of them seemed any longer of any real consequence. I didn't know whether Freud grew more interested. I tried hard to think of real problems I had had.

October 15, 1934

This was another uneventful hour. Freud moved into his city home (IX Berggasse 19) over the weekend, and I went there for the first time today: a simple Viennese residence on the first floor of an ordinary house, in an ordinary part of Vienna. There was a butcher-shop downstairs. The entrance was dilapidated, like most entrances in Vienna during that period. Upstairs there was a glass plate on the door with "Prof. Dr. Freud 3-4" on it. . . . I was admitted to a cozy, simple but somewhat cluttered waiting room whose walls were covered with pictures, diplomas, and honorary degrees from many lands. Among the pictures was an excellent one of Havelock Ellis in his prime, sitting back at his desk, with folded arms and clear eyes. There was an inscription on it: "With sincere regards and admiration." Among the books was the Goldberg biography of Ellis, likewise inscribed from Ellis to "Professor Freud." Among the pictures were several group photos taken at Clark University in 1909 with Stanley Hall, Freud, and Jung in the foreground. There was an assortment of other miscellaneous books in all languages (including Chinese) and on all subjects, many of them inscribed in flattering terms to Freud: Woodworth's book *Contemporary Schools of Psychology*, H.D.'s poems, Calverton's book on sex, Malinowski in German, *Das Geschlechtsleben in Japan, Mein Weltbild* by Einstein, *The Old School* collection of essays, as well as the hand-press Joseph Ishill volume on Ellis with a simple inscription from the printer. None of the books looked as if they were much read.

Freud was again mild, earnest and friendly when I came in. "These are our new quarters," he said.

I made some remark about the Ellis picture, but he did not respond, and I went on with my account of myself. I had been walking in the country the day before, and was in good shape and spirits. I continued with the history of my vicissitudes in love and life, making the last years short, for the amount of personal history one could tell seemed endless, and I wanted to get on. I succeeded in concluding the brief account of my life from adolescence on, and planned to continue with an account of my childhood. I made some reference to his earlier remark that my account was uninteresting. Freud explained that he had not meant he was uninterested, but that he thought I was, because I kept speaking of clear, superficial things. I explained that it was not exactly uninteresting to me, but that generally I found that

I was not very contented when I was overconcerned with myself and that I might also have a certain amount of apprehension about the course the analysis would take and what unpleasantness it would reveal.

"But today," I said, "I feel more sure and confident of myself and await results with more equanimity."

Freud seemed attentive, but, as usual, said next to nothing, beyond making occasional brief comments: "For so long?," "With her?," etc., or laughing quietly when I said something funny. Once he asked, "What did you live on all this time?"

I again spoke a little of Ellis and mentioned casually that he had suggested in a letter I just received that I might find it useful to look up Wilhelm Stekel too while I was in Vienna. The hour passed quickly, as usual, and I was stopped at the end.

October 16, 1934

My good spirits continued. There was considerable conversation between us today and we got into sharp discussion. It began by my mentioning that I had been reading from the Schizophrenia volume in the Bumke *Handbuch der Psychiatrie,* and felt satisfaction in seeing that my own conclusions about schizophrenia coincided with the author's: it was not a disease entity, but a symptom complex of a group of diseases with some common features.

Freud remonstrated: the cause of schizophrenia was still unknown; it was not a symptom, it was a syndrome, like hysteria. In short, it seemed, as I later recalled what was said, that Freud was irritated that I should air independent views somewhat at variance with his own, and that I should moreover explain away my own problems to my own satisfaction.

He addressed me: "I have noticed, during your recitation up to now, a special characteristic: a tendency to leave the solid ground of facts, and to talk in a general way of things that are not intelligible to me. You talk away, for example, of your feelings and experiences without so much as telling me where and when they all occurred. Furthermore, I have been able to observe in you a tendency to lose yourself in abstractions and to talk of things of which you have no knowledge, in a way which reminds me of someone whom I know, Havelock Ellis. He speaks freely of things about which he has no knowledge at all without so much as concerning himself with the literature. How a man with any knowledge of things could ever have recommended you to Stekel"—Freud was referring to the fact that yesterday's letter from Ellis had done this—"is beyond my comprehension."

He then said some very harsh things of Stekel: a man of no scruples, with no regard for others, of the meanest ambitions, with petty ideas of grandeur (*"mit erbsengrossem Grössenwahn,"* if I remember him correctly; I am at least sure he used the word *erbsengross,* which means "the size of a pea") . . . whose behavior was such "that it was impossible to have any further relations with him."

Freud seemed piqued, and piqued with a matter which apparently had no close relation to my analysis. It seemed so irrelevant that I was only slightly disconcerted but at once said a few things in self-defense and explanation: that I was sorry if I said or supposed anything that was untrue, but since I was asked at the outset to tell of everything that went through my head, it is not surprising if a lot of nonsense came out. Regarding schizophrenia, my main point was that I was originally told that schizophrenia was nothing but an extreme form of schizoid personality, and hence not sharply differentiated from the normal. Since I had come to the independent conclusion that this view was incorrect, I came to look upon schizophrenia as a disease like pneumonia or diabetes which might strike one or not, but did not necessarily have any close relation to people's daily troubles. For the rest, I had no ambition to erect eternal scientific truths, but recognized that everything changes, and my views would change in time too.

Freud was sympathetic to all this, agreed with me, urged me to continue to speak out my own thoughts freely, and I went on, first finishing the main points of my *Lebenslauf* from puberty to now, by mentioning some more or less casual boy-girl affairs I had. "You might otherwise have the impression," I said, "that I had very few such relations."

"Do you consider it important, then, to have many such affairs?" he asked.

"By no means," I said. "It was simply because I could find no satisfactory mate all this time."

"Exactly," he said.

I then described my early home life and boyhood. "It was on the whole a very happy one," I said, "and I think, all things considered, I had a very fortunate and sensible upbringing."

"I am very glad to hear that," said Freud, "for it is certainly unusual."

I then briefly described my early life at home and at public school, up to the time I entered high school. It was a little past my hour when Freud said it would be a convenient place to stop.

"I have listened," he said, when he gave me his hand. "*Ich habe zugehört.*"

Yesterday's hour was pleasant and informal. Freud's dog, the handsome chow, was in the hall when I came in, and the maid told me it was the professor's great favorite. "The Herr Professor is very much attached to it," she said; "when the dog doesn't eat, the Herr Professor is unhappy." The dog and I were both admitted at the same time.

I spoke a little of politics this time, for it occupied my mind, and Freud seemed interested, though noncommittal. Regarding Communism, I said, it sometimes seemed that if you were not for it, you were against it. "Precisely," he said.

I then said that his criticism of me yesterday ought to disqualify me as a scientist, but I didn't take it too seriously.

"I simply said you had a certain undesirable *tendency* (*Neigung*)," said Freud.

"In any case," I said, "since you said Ellis had the same defect, I feel I am at least in good company."

"That's right—*Eben*," said Freud.

I resumed the account of my early childhood. Freud asked particularly precise questions about early sexual experiences. I led up to my first social experience with a girl, when at the age of fourteen I took her to the theater.

"That," I said, "was my first . . ."

"*Abenteuer*," suggested Freud, and the hour thus ended with my first adventure.

Today I finished the main points in my account of myself, and proceeded to tell of my dreams. That was what Freud was waiting for.

"There are people who cannot be analyzed, often perfectly normal people," he said, "and I have been waiting up to now to see if you would tell me of your dreams, because that is how we shall now proceed with the analysis. That is how I analyzed myself, by studying my own dreams over a period of three years. The next few days will show whether enough material for an analysis will be forthcoming."

I told him that I dreamt I had embraced his servant girl and that he was scandalized.

"That dream," he said, "is not of much importance, but we shall see."

October 19, 1934

I dreamt last night that I was asked to visit Ellis and Françoise (I interpreted this as a simple wish), and found myself on a curving road overlooking a valley en route to their home which I saw in the distance beyond some trees and bushes. The scene was a typical English countryside resembling a resort, Burling Gap, where I had spent some time. I was a little too early, since I was not to come before twelve, and rested by the roadside before moving on. (This corresponded to a previous actual experience.) I saw Françoise and Havelock in the distance, and could tell from their movements that they had seen me. I heard Françoise cry to her son François, "What is Wortis's first name again?" and he told her "Joseph." I then arrived. There were numerous visitors about, including a plump French sister of Françoise. Françoise greeted me and seemed actually to want to kiss me, though I moved on. Havelock had a haircut. Before arriving, I had wondered to myself whether he would have long straggling hair (like a certain eccentric who walks about in Vienna). I was cordially and quietly greeted by Havelock. It was growing foggy and dark. "It is nothing but the English mists," said Havelock.

"But upon the hill, before I came down, it was perfectly clear," I said.

"The fog settles in the valleys," he said.

I stood at the entrance porch of the house, and a whole file of foreign-looking men, kitchen help, walked past me through the door, while their wives entered the kitchen door down below.

"How in the world will so many people get into this small house?" I thought. "The house will burst." This last thought was so disturbing that I awakened. I was eager to find out what Freud would make of it.

At the analytic hour I told Freud of my dream, and also gave my interpretations: The commotion on my arrival in the dream corresponded to a previous real experience, and Françoise's concern about my name reflected a real situation too, because she used to make repeated friendly efforts to call me by my first name, only to lapse into the use of my second name again, for which she would apologize. The many visitors about reflected a wish of mine that Ellis, like Goethe, would move in society, and the presence of a plump French sister of Françoise was an invention to create an atmosphere of domesticity. The business of Françoise wanting to kiss me represented a notion that her interest in me had a sexual element. Havelock's haircut reflected a wish that he would be more conventional, and not eccentric. The discussion about the fogginess and darkness was partly a pedantic attempt at conversational realism, but also reflected, I thought, a rationalization of the physiological process which tends to make dreams so often seem dark.

Freud now proceeded to give me my first real lesson in analysis. Some of the things were correctly interpreted, he said. Other things were hidden from me because of my preconceived scientific opinions or prejudices. The dream was an *anxiety dream*, and since the only abnormal thing that had come up was the hypochondriacal idea, it was concerned with that. My future instruction would have the purpose of removing my scientific prejudices.

I had also had another short dream: that some small animals approached my bed, and that a kitten licked and chewed at my little finger. I could not interpret this, but supposed that I had my finger caught somewhere in the bed or cover, and that this was a rationalization of the sensations I felt.

Freud remonstrated: "I thought that theory was a *chose jugée—a settled matter*." He used the French and English phrases. "It was all fully discussed in my book long ago. . . . Such things may provide the *occasion* for a dream but do not explain the content." Concerning other assumptions of mine —that, for example, the associative processes in dreams are disturbed—he said this did not accord with psychoanalytic views. Regarding the matter of the darkness in the first dream, he considered that an ominous foreboding of the end the dream would take.

When Freud said part of my dream material could not be interpreted because my scientific beliefs acted as *Widerstand*, I asked whether it is *always* possible to interpret dreams where there is no *Widerstand*.

"For the wealth of possible associations is so great," I said, "that there may well be technical difficulties in interpreting a dream."

"There is no such thing," said Freud. He seemed to have great faith in free association.

I then began to ask questions. The first question was whether the analyst undertakes to be honest too, as his patient does.

"He does not," said Freud, mistakenly thinking I was referring to the case histories in his own writing; "the analyst practices discretion in his reports or studies."

"But does he practice honesty with the patient?," I asked.

Freud replied, I believe, that the analyst uses tact. "He does not lie," said Freud, "for then the patient, and other patients, would lose faith in him and mistrust him. That is why children mistrust their parents, because of the sex lies that were told them."

Suppose, I said, a patient were a severe neurotic, an incurable case, would Freud tell him so?

"You mean, do I think you are neurotic," he said.

I laughed, and said I didn't think I meant that; I didn't consider myself neurotic and didn't think I would be. At the worst, I was concerned to know whether Freud considered me neurotic, but I had not intended to ask him. I continued to talk freely. He would either say I was not neurotic, in which case I would agree, or that I was neurotic, in which case I would feel obliged to disagree. For the rest, when was one to call a person neurotic? I was pleasantly occupied, well able to work and enjoy myself, and did not seem to have any great present troubles. When I told Freud at the first hour we had, that I had had some disconcerting ideas some months ago, which disappeared in time, he was sceptical.

"It is impossible," he repeated.

So that, I continued, I had to take the view that Freud believed I was still troubled by these ideas. Since a patient, in one sense or another, comes to a doctor for reassurance, I wondered whether he had done the right thing. Doesn't it sometimes happen that a difficulty of that sort disappears by itself?

"It does happen, of course," he said, "but it is liable to recur."

"But if it disappeared the first time, wouldn't it disappear the second time too?" I asked.

"That is a scholastic question (*eine Doktorfrage*)," said Freud. "It may come back again and again, unless it is thoroughly analyzed. Everybody has some such little trouble. You just had some little phobia. Everybody has some neurotic traits."

So that I felt I had not come off so badly after all. "A little phobia," and in the past tense too, and "the only abnormal thing" . . . all this seemed fair and true, and perhaps flattering. Freud himself (in *Über Deckerinnerungen*) said that he had a *"kleine Phobie"* (he described himself transparently there as a "38-year-old *Akademiker"*). My self-esteem was not completely blasted, and there seemed to be enough healthy stuff left, even in Freud's opinion, to live on contentedly.

October 22, 1934

Today's hour was most productive. Freud was in a friendly mood and talked freely. I was somewhat under the weather. Freud supposed it was due to the conflict with my unconscious he had aroused, but I said I thought it was due to more immediate troubles, with my work, and with my still uncertain future. Furthermore I was in a physically neglected state. I told Freud that I was not displeased with having a little phobia, although I added I was not altogether convinced I had one; it was just one of a series of disagreeable thoughts I sometimes had about myself, but which I did not take too seriously. I was inclined to criticize myself severely,

37

and often wondered whether I was *vollwertig,* or up to expectations.

"That is perfectly natural for a young person who has not yet tried his strength," said Freud. "All young people should feel that way; if they do not it is abnormal. But it is irrelevant whether you have a phobia now or not. Phobias are very common and I have had three or four myself; it is in any case an interesting point which ought to be examined."

Before proceeding with the analysis, I asked whether I could from time to time discuss more general questions with him, which had no direct bearing on the analysis. Under the terms of my fellowship I was, for example, expected sooner or later to study the problem of homosexuality, and it would be interesting to know whether he thought that constitutional factors were important in its causation.

"They are so very striking (*so ins Auge springend*) I haven't the least doubt of their importance," said Freud, "and certain types, northern Europeans for example, seem to be especially predisposed."

"And yet," I said, "it has flourished most in southern countries, in ancient Persia and Greece for example, and had disappeared again with changing fashions, though the racial continuity was preserved."

"That is still an unsettled problem," he said, "though it is true that certain cultures may promote the development of homosexuality."

"In any case," I said, "it is clear I have to study the constitution of homosexuals too."

"I should think so," he said, "though it is another question whether you will find anything."

"There were times in the past when I used to wonder whether I was manly enough," I said.

"Nobody is completely masculine," said Freud.

"Years ago I used to think my voice was perhaps too high," I said, "though it is lower now."

Freud reminded me that one of my teachers at Bellevue, Schilder, a psychoanalyst, had a very high voice. I said I had noticed it and had thought about it. Freud hadn't known that Ellis's voice was rather high. I said it seemed to be frequently associated with a certain amount of tenseness which is often encountered in people of high ability. I was inclined to think it was a result of simple muscular tension affecting the vocal chords.

"I don't know about that," said Freud.

"At least I have observed in myself," I said, "that my voice is deep when I am relaxed—in a warm bath, for example—and higher when I am under tension, among strangers for example. It is at least true as far as I am concerned," I concluded.

"Don't say things in that way," said Freud; "it makes a bad impression."

I apologized, and said I simply meant that the observation held good for me, though maybe not for others.

"And this brings us to the dream you had," said Freud, "for I have observed certain feminine elements in it—which by no means implies that you are effeminate," he added. He then said, "The analyst does not say all that he thinks, but lets the subject talk until he reaches a point or topic that can be used in the analysis."

One of the feminine elements in my dream, according to Freud, was the symbolic entry of the line of servants into the house. This, thought Freud, might represent a mother's womb with my brother and sisters issuing from it. Similarly, the dream of the little animals sucking my finger might have

39

represented female elements (since little animals always meant females) sucking at the breast. Ellis and Françoise represented my father and mother, and my disinclination to kiss her meant I really wanted to, and it was an Oedipus symbol. I thought this last was quite likely, but said that I thought the other things seemed far-fetched. Furthermore, since I felt no anxiety in the dream itself, I did not feel sure it was an anxiety dream.

"You awakened before the actual anxiety came," said Freud. "For the present," he added, "we are simply working with suppositions, since the analysis has only just begun."

I ventured to say that I felt many dreams were simply a rationalization of a prevailing mood of the dreamer.

"It is more likely to be just the contrary," said Freud, "and the dream represents a mood which the subject does not allow himself when awake." He said, in addition, that it was not good to have preconceived ideas, since I would in time find I would have to revise them when I examined my dreams.

When the subject of encephalitis happened to be mentioned, Freud handed me a medical journal he had just received from Istanbul which he had in his hand, opened on an article called "Encephalitis" with some pictures of Freud. He was obviously thinking of telepathy. "The man who sent this to me from Istanbul five days ago could not have known of our conversation in advance. But," he said, "coincidences are always possible." I said Ellis believed in the possibility of telepathy but thought it was difficult to demonstrate.

I told Freud we were thinking of having a child; my wife and I were talking about it but we were still undecided.

"But your wife, who is twenty-eight, ought to have her children now while she is young."

"I shall tell her that," I said. "I know she'll be very glad to hear that Professor Freud thinks so."

"It's no piece of wisdom on my part," said Freud. "It is just ordinary medical knowledge that childbirth after thirty is no easy matter for a woman, merely from a physical point of view."

Freud again found occasion to speak strongly against Stekel. "Stekel," he said, "goes about and tells the patient at the outset: 'You hate your father, you have a fixation on your mother, etc.' which only arouses the patient's antagonisms. Next time you write to Ellis, tell him that he really should be ashamed of himself (*er soll sich wirklich schämen*) that he recommended Stekel to you in any sense whatsoever."

October 23, 1934

Today's hour was unsatisfactory. I was physically fatigued, mildly depressed, and rather indifferent, tired of boring into my interior. I spoke of various other things. I had been looking into Professor Krauss's *Geschlechtsleben in Japan* and asked Freud what he thought of it. He thought it a sober and valuable book; (Ellis, I think, had called it pornographic). I spoke of Hirschfeld. Freud said he knew him well, and that Hirschfeld was well informed, but scientifically dumb (*wissenschaftlich dumm*). I said he seemed to be homosexual himself.

"He doesn't *seem* to be," said Freud, "he *is*, and he makes no secret of it. And not only is he homosexual, but he is perverted in other ways. I have heard from a patient of mine how he satisfies himself in the most perverted way." This was said with emphasis, almost as if in moral indignation, and I did not know how it accorded with Freud's views on the analyst's discretion. I said a homosexual was not likely to write objectively on homosexuality, but Freud thought he might very well be able to shed light on the subject.

Soon afterwards I brought up the question of the future of monogamy under socialism. What did psychoanalysis think of it? Freud said it was a social question to which psychoanalysis can give no answer.

"You must not expect that psychoanalysis gives finished answers to questions, which you can then take back home with you. All it can do is give insight into certain facts, and the problems are solved by the patient. We don't know what the future of monogamy will be, and cannot prophesy. There are places in the world today where monogamy is not practiced. If socialism comes, we shall see what happens. It is useless to prophesy. Monogamy does not seem to be disappearing in Russia. Monogamy in Europe today," said Freud, "is a very loose affair anyway."

We spoke of conditions in Russia for a while: I said the tendencies there are not clear, and the old morality certainly survives. "Still," I said, "there may be strong psychoanalytic reasons for the continuance of monogamy. If a person looks for a mother type and finds one, perhaps he will be permanently satisfied."

"That is by no means clear," said Freud, "for Don Juanism is connected with a mother fixation too."

I resumed my account of myself, and said that in past years I had experience with both steady and sporadic relationships, thought that each had special attractions and shortcomings, but that I now found monogamy satisfactory.

I gave an account of a dream I had last night in which two Negroes fought with each other and one was shot. I said I had been hearing talk of the oncoming revolution the night before and found it disturbing, and thought the dream represented a symbol of strife and bloodshed. I had no definite associations for various details in the dream, at least apparently none that seemed significant.

I had occasion to mention a dream I had long ago regarding *The Hairy Ape* of Eugene O'Neill and I told Freud of the scene in the play where the hero, a stoker, releases the ape from its cage and is then crushed to death by it.

"That would be more appropriately a dream about the revolution," Freud said; "you, as a member of the bourgeoisie—which you are—free the worker, only to be killed by him."

I also had a dream that same night involving intimacies with a girl acquaintance. I could find no specially significant associations there either. I said in the course of the discussion of the dream that I preferred a "common sense" psychology. Freud then said I had too many ideas and too few associations. Either I could not relax myself sufficiently or else I had tremendous resistance (*riesige Widerstände*). I did however discuss various memories and details, and Freud said in conclusion, "We have moved a little forward."

October 24, 1934

Today I had to leave an absorbing lecture on neuropathology to go to Freud's. I started the hour by saying that I had just left an interesting lecture on pathology at the Neurological Institute where I was working. I said I liked that kind of work, and if I had absolutely free rein that was what I would be doing, studying the organic basis of mental function.

"I should think you might," said Freud, and then added sharply that I seemed to have more talent for that than for this sort of thing. I was a little surprised and hurt, perhaps a little amused that Freud should suddenly say that, and I said at once that I was sorry he thought so. Perhaps I ought to change my work, I suggested.

Freud made a little speech. "A person who professes to believe in common sense psychology and who thinks psychoanalysis is 'far-fetched' can certainly have no understanding of it, for it is common sense which produces all the ills we have to cure."

I explained that I simply meant that I preferred a psychology to be as simple as possible, and that I did not imply a criticism in saying his interpretation of a house as a womb was "far-fetched." I had simply meant to explain why I could not easily see the connection between the two. Freud said that the simpler a psychology was, the less likely it was to be true. There was no need to change my profession, or to stop the analysis, since I could in any case learn something from it.

"Besides," I said. "how do you know I would do any better in neurology? A fact is a fact in any subject, and if I don't grasp facts perhaps I am no good at all."

"It is just a question of suitability to the work," said Freud. "I have seen a lot of ambitious young people, and I can tell from their reaction how they will turn out. It is simply a matter of vocational choice."

"That is too bad," I said, "since I shall probably continue my work in psychology anyway. I consider you the greatest psychologist we have had, and I should have liked nothing better than a word of encouragement from you. I'm sorry I have got just the opposite."

"There is no need to show *you* any consideration," said Freud. "You have a degree of self-confidence that fortifies you against criticism. It is really enviable."

I said a few words about the encouragement Ellis had

given me. "Ellis's interest in you was just part of his general kindness," said Freud.

"Don't you think Ellis has any talent for psychology, either?" I asked.

"He certainly hasn't," said Freud. "I was reading his book on dreams last night. It has good ideas here and there, but the book as a whole does not show much insight. Stekel, at least, in spite of his faults, had a certain gift for association and combination, and we are indebted to him for some valuable symbol interpretations. For the rest, you have yourself told me how easily you learn things, and so on."

I said I didn't feel self-satisfied myself—quite the contrary —but I supposed it was a relative term, and it might be that I plagued myself less than others. Ellis thought that I had too little self-assurance.

"You belong to the group of happy people," said Freud. "You have your little fluctuations as young people do, but you are essentially happy." I tried to explain how sorry I was he got these impressions, that I regretted I had so much *Widerstand* and that I had acquired prejudices; I was quite willing to abandon them though I was obliged to acknowledge them while they were there.

I proceeded to recount a dream: that I had mounted a ladder to get two books down from some library shelves, in the presence of Professor Marburg, to give to some woman doctor in the background. I said I felt it simply meant that I was climbing to get something that the Professor (Freud) could not get because of his age. Freud had me associate some of the things in the dream, and finally concluded that the ladder meant coitus, the books meant women, and the woman in the background was my wife. I was showing the old Professor, in short, how well I could practice coitus, to the annoyance of my wife. "That sounds at least plausible," he concluded, and I agreed. When I shook hands to leave I said again I hoped he would change his opinion of me in time and would tell me when he did, so that I could repress the memory of what he said today.

"No need for that," he said.

As I left I asked whether he used the terms psychoanalysis and psychology interchangeably.

"It's the same thing," he said. "All psychology is psycho-analysis; what is left is the physiology of the senses."

October 25, 1934

A letter from Ellis arrived, with the following pertinent references:

23 October, 1934
Haslemere

DEAR JOSEPH:

Your letters are interesting and I trust all goes well with your Freud experience, which certainly cannot fail to prove instructive (I have heard nothing lately from ———; some time ago, as I may have mentioned to you, he asked me to *cable* him if I thought Freudian analysis was *necessary* for you; I did not do so, but wrote that I thought it advantageous but not necessary). It certainly seems desirable to have made clear at the outset to him what your attitude is. It seems to me that his resentment is always directed mainly against those who were once declared disciples and then left him, and that he is not so very hostile to those who have never been his disciples. I rather wonder what he now says of Rank who was for so many years so closely associated with him, and is now completely emancipated (in some ways, it seems to me, rather in the direction of Jung). He has lately shown me two chapters of a new and much re-written version of his "*Incest-Motif.*" He very much dissolves Freud's conception of the Oedipus Complex. You would certainly find Rank interesting to read, apart from any question of agreement; his culture is so wide and his literary style so good (not so always his translator's).

What you say of the decay of the conventional distinction between psychological and physical is certainly true. I am always coming across evidence of it in all sorts of biological (and also philosophical) directions. Only this morning, again, when chancing to look into Ortega y Gasset . . .

Affectionately,
HAVELOCK

The letter contained other references to scientific discussions of ours with both agreements and disagreements, all in a tone of friendly debate which contrasted sharply with my current scientific discussions in Vienna.

When I came for my analytic hour Freud found me reading, as usual, in his waiting room when he came in. "You can borrow any books you like," he said, "only you must tell me when you do."

I began my hour by saying that I still felt offended at what he said yesterday. "Self-complacency and lack of talent are a bad combination," I said, "and I don't feel flattered."

"They often occur together," said Freud, "but I didn't mean to pass final judgment on you. I still don't know you well enough. If Ellis for example were to write to me, 'What do you think of Wortis?', I should answer that I had not known him long enough to say."

I protested that psychoanalysts too often made use of the

convenient *argumentum ad hominem* to dispose of their critics, but that I thought it was bad scientific practice.

Freud agreed. "It's true," he said, "that the young analysts analyze too much. But I was using the method in private, in the course of an analysis, to remove *Widerstand*, though it was appropriate just the same."

"But you simply increase the *Widerstand* by such methods," I said.

"That would just be a personal *Widerstand*," said Freud, "and would be easy to dispose of."

I proceeded to give an account of two dreams I had, both of them concerned with failure and loss of libido. Freud went back to another dream I had recounted yesterday, though, about a former teacher, and my guilt feelings in the dream for being truant from school. We discussed various free associations to the dream, and whether certain numbers in the dream were concerned with money or not. Finally, Freud hit the sofa and said, "I have an idea! But I don't know whether it will please you. Or rather I don't care whether it pleases you; I don't know whether it is appropriate to the dream." He suggested that the dream meant that I was thinking of making money by absenting myself from the analysis now and then, and keeping the money for myself. I said I didn't think the interpretation applicable, since the idea had never even remotely occurred to me. Freud then took pains to explain to me that I would actually have to pay in any case whether I came every day or not. This was said in earnest. Freud then asked me about my private finances, and whether the continuance of my analysis was in any way endangered. I assured him it was not.

I had told the servant girl when I came in that the Professor had been angry with me yesterday, but she said it didn't sound like him. "I've been working here so long," she said, "and I've never seen the Herr Professor really angry." She asked me when I left if the Professor was still angry with me, but I said he was much nicer today.

October 26, 1934

I started the hour by speaking in a general way about things I had been reading in neurology, and said I was much interested in the relation between analysis and the conditioned reflex. But no comment was made, and I went on to recite a dream in which I visited an old girl friend. But I could not help reminding myself, in the course of my account, of Freud's recent remarks, and since I was told to go on and tell my thoughts, I said that it was regrettable— *bedauerlich*—that Freud was so intolerant toward critics. "You act as if psychoanalysis stood high and perfect, and only our own faults keep us from accepting it; it does not seem to occur to you that it is simply polite to reckon with one's own prejudices too."

"An analysis is not a place for polite exchanges," said Freud. "I observed that you had a certain amount of *Widerstand* and set about to remove it."

"I can't see the technical advantage of that," I said, "for my pleasure in analysis is certainly diminished."

"It is best to leave matters of technique to me," said Freud.

"I don't see why you brought Ellis in and slighted his relation to me," I went on to say. "Ellis is your loyal friend, and would be saddened to hear what you said of him."

"I think he knows what I think of him," said Freud. "I don't know why he is interested in you—I have no information on the subject—I just said it was a *sign* of his general kindness."

We continued to talk in this petty way for a good part of the hour, since Freud seemed to insist on my complying with the rule to say everything I thought. I do not think he was indifferent to my remarks, though he sometimes took offense at the wrong things. I said, for example, that my wife suggested that maybe I was being oversensitive.

"You will please tell your wife that I can make my own observations," he said. "If she were to come here, I should probably be very polite to her, but the analysis is a private matter between you and me, and you ought not to speak to anyone about it. You want to learn more about human nature (*Menschenkenntnis*) because you are ignorant and I am here to teach you. An analysis is not a chivalrous affair between two equals." On the whole, Freud seemed contained and conciliatory, but my own feelings were unpleasant in more than one way, and I was dejected when I left.

"On Monday, again," said Freud.

October 29, 1934

I took advantage of Freud's permission to read his works again. He had originally said it would interfere with the analysis, but he said on Friday I might just as well, since I had read so much anyway. I read from his introductory *Vorlesungen* and various essays with great interest and admiration, and commenced my hour yesterday by saying so.

"There have been few men in the history of science who produced something of such real importance so independently," I said.

"I had my predecessors," said Freud, but he was apparently not displeased.

"As for me," I said, "I must say again that I am sorry if I have been stubborn and superior, and make slow headway in accepting your ideas. Conceit is an unpleasant quality: I don't like it in others, and I am sure they don't like it in me. I should be perfectly willing if you treat it as a bad symptom and cure it if you can."

"I shall tell you when it comes up," said Freud.

"It was not so much your criticisms I minded," I said, "as the feeling that I was not liked."

"I didn't mean to put my personal feelings into it," said Freud, and the discussion was therewith closed in a pleasant atmosphere.

The dreams I had to report were three in number, and were concerned with my disappointment or sorrow at the loss of love in one form or another, which I related—correctly, said Freud—to our little unpleasant experience. I was then at a loss how to go on, and the question of my old phobia was revived. I repeated my story once more, and again said in all honesty that it no longer troubled me, though it was associated with unpleasant recollections.

"It is a reminiscence," said Freud. "I feel," he went on, "that this phobia, or concern of yours is worth going into. Something may be behind it."

He agreed some overconcern about health was especially common among students who start work in medicine. "But it has a reason," he added.

I declared my willingness to admit this, and said I had some qualms about boring (*grübeln*) into it.

"It's not boring into it," said Freud. The revival of this old worry left me saddened and subdued, but I was glad the atmosphere had changed.

Freud spoke of the word "introversion" I had used. He said it was not a psychoanalytic term, but was invented by Jung and was often misused. Its appropriate use, he explained, was for extreme loss of interest in the outside world, as in schizophrenia; but everybody had a certain degree of introversion and extroversion. Freud some time before had also objected to the concept of "schizoid personality" as evolved by Kretschmer. "It is simply a kind of character development," said Freud, and implied it had no close relation to schizophrenia, though I am not sure he actually said this. He also spoke on a little technical matter: remembering dreams. One should make no special effort to remember them, he said, and it is futile to note them down at the bedside with pencil and paper. By trying too hard, the resistance is simply moved to the side to cover something else, and it was in any case significant to note what was remembered most easily. If one has a natural interest and pleasure in thinking of a dream, that is another matter.

October 31, 1934

We came to discuss the question of the conditioned reflex again yesterday. "The concept belongs to physiology," said Freud, "It is silly (*lächerlich*) to try to explain neuroses by it. Give me an example!"

I gave the example of Browning's persistent unwillingness to return to his old home after his mother's death, "because," I said, "it was simply associated with an unpleasant experience."

"But many people *refuse* to leave the scene of a beloved person's death," said Freud. "Why is that? It's not so simple. Browning's reaction was abnormal, and it would be important to ask why. Why was he so attached to his mother? Why did he react in that special way?" I also spoke of the frequency of early initiation into homosexual experiences among people who later became homosexual. Freud quoted Ellis to the effect that there must have been a special susceptibility in these people, or else they would not have responded. "There are all sorts of additional factors: *When* the experience occurred, under what circumstances, to what individual, and so on. The idea of the conditioned reflex is completely superfluous. These are all merely associations," continued Freud, "not reflexes; a reflex is an extremely simple matter. Rous, the pathologist, showed that when you injure an embryo in a very early stage you produce severe pathological changes in the animal later. If you injure it at a later stage you get much less striking changes."

I also brought up the question of the importance of constitution, and said I was glad he had written that half of every neurosis was organic.

"I wrote nothing of the sort," he said. "What I wrote was that the greater the organic disposition was, the less the psychological trauma has to be, and vice versa, and that there was a whole series of degrees (*Ergänzungsreihe*) in which the combinations varied."

I again told of the contact I had with a relative who became insane when I was a boy, and Freud thought it was significant. My parents should not have allowed us children to see that sort of thing, he said. I also said that the peculiar distaste people feel about going insane as compared with some other illness was due to the idea that they would become laughable in the eyes of others.

"That," he said, "is a valuable suggestion, *ein wichtiger Beitrag.*"

I again began to speak of past unhappiness, but said I disliked reviving all this. "Don't you think you can revive past troubles in an analysis, without relieving them?" I asked.

"Nothing is revived," said Freud. "Everything comes from within the patient. If he has any problem within him, naturally it would revive itself, and would be uprooted."

The hour was over. Before going, I spoke of some discussion I had had with Professor Julius Bauer, the internist, on a question of psychology, in which I supported some claim of Freud's. "But you must learn to quote me correctly," said Freud. (*"Sie müssen mich aber richtig zitieren lernen."*)

November 1, 1934

I had been reading *Zur Einführung des Narzissmus* and had a few questions ready for Freud.

"What *is* a neurosis?" I asked. "What is the difference between neuroses and ordinary troubles? Can a person feel well and still be neurotic?"

"That would be unlikely," said Freud. "At best, he can tolerate his neurosis and get along. There are disorders of character, too," said Freud, "which are not neuroses but which may be unpleasant for the patient."

"Not in themselves, though," I suggested. "For a quality of character cannot be bad in itself unless it is unpleasant for society, which then makes it unpleasant for the person."

"Yes," said Freud, and he then gave a rather complete and formal definition of character as "the sum of all the regularly recurring reactions of an individual."

"Then both neuroses and faults of character are fit objects for psychoanalytic treatment."

"Yes."

"Napoleon then," I suggested, "might be analyzed even though he might be happy."

"Yes," said Freud.

"That is a sensitive spot with me," I said, "for I sometimes think I may have faults of character."

"It doesn't matter in analysis," said Freud. "We are not here to judge, not even if you were a criminal, or for my part a saint.

"Some people are simply unsuited for analysis—*ungeeignet*," said Freud. "I don't know whether you have ever examined protozoa under the microscope. Some animals are completely transparent, others are opaque, even though they only consist of a single cell like the others: they have too much pigment in them. Some people are like that too, and one cannot see through them."

"There are plenty of people who are ready to call any unusual behavior neurotic," I said, "like the students at my college who thought there must be something wrong with anybody who read poetry."

"Unusual conduct isn't necessarily neurotic," said Freud.

"Many people take it for granted, too," I said, "that homosexuals are neurotic, though they might be perfectly capable of leading happy and quiet lives if society would tolerate them."

"No psychoanalyst has ever claimed that homosexuals cannot be perfectly decent people," said Freud. "Psychoanalysis does not undertake to judge people in any case."

"Still," I said, "it makes a difference to homosexuals whether they are considered neurotic or not."

"Naturally homosexuality is something pathological," said Freud. "It is an arrested development (*eine Entwicklungshemmung*)."

"But plenty of valuable qualities could be called the same: you might call the simplicity of genius a kind of childishness or arrested development too," I said.

"Of course," said Freud, "the fact that a person is a genius doesn't prevent his having pathological traits: if he is only five feet tall instead of six, that would have to be called pathological."

"The question, though," I said, "is whether one ought to undertake to *cure* homosexuals as if they were diseased, or make their lot easier by making society more tolerant."

"Naturally," said Freud, "the emphasis ought to be put on social measures; the only homosexuals one can attempt to cure are those who want to be changed."

"But that might only have the effect of making them discontented heterosexuals instead of honest homosexuals."

"Certainly," said Freud. "One often has the experience of starting an analysis with a homosexual who then finds such relief in being and talking just as he is that he drops the analysis and remains homosexual."

"Another question I wanted to ask is how important you have found money troubles in the etiology of neuroses? You do not seem to consider that in your writings, and I would be curious to know how you feel about it."

Freud seemed to take unnecessary offense at this. "There are a lot of things I don't mention in my books," he said. "That's the sort of criticism I often hear from the Bolsheviki. I can't discuss everything. I don't discuss climate either, though it is certainly important. I should certainly feel better if I were in a better climate. Certainly money troubles contribute to neuroses. Many things do. You might just as well criticize a chemist for not writing about physics. These are all such unimportant problems you bring up, the kind of easy questions that ought not to interest a serious scientist at all."

I said I was sorry: I knew the questions were simple and naïve; that was why I wanted to settle them at the outset.

"We don't settle them," said Freud, "we disregard them. I don't understand how you can concern yourself with such purely conventional problems (*rein konventionelle Probleme*), what is a neurosis and what is not a neurosis, what is pathological or not pathological—all mere words—fights about words. First learn something about neuroses and then you will know what a neurosis is. With all your scientific curiosity (*Wissbegierde*) there are big loopholes in your interests. Your business is to learn something about yourself. You talk of this and that, about money and abstract questions, because you are not really interested in yourself—you have no curiosity. You have too many of what you yourself call prejudices. I remember them all, and will recite them to you in time. First, your famous 'common sense,' then your 'far-fetched,' then—I forget what—."

"Conditioned reflex," I suggested.

"Yes, conditioned reflex—such nonsense—when my friend Bechterev thinks he can explain everything with conditioned reflexes; and then yesterday you brought up the most important of all—the '*sleeping dog*' (in English)—one ought not to awaken him." I think Freud was here referring to the English saying, "Let sleeping dogs lie." "It does sometimes happen that a normal person can start a psychoanalysis and become neurotic in the course of it, and then be cured," he added. "But that is only because he carries the germ of a neurosis in him. You are not neurotic, but you can be in time. The thing to do is to bring it all out and uproot it. That is what you don't want to do, and all other reasons are just a cover for this."

"That is quite possible," I said. "I am perhaps afraid of my unconscious."

"Of course," said Freud, "that is why you make all these

57

difficulties. I tell you, it may be just as well if we make this our last hour"—he had given me the month's bill at the outset—"if you feel that way about it."

I said I would be sorry if the analysis had to stop. I would do what I could to cooperate and would always be ready to change my views.

"All right," said Freud, "but you ought to be ashamed of yourself for acting that way, grumbling and growling for three days because I said this or that to you. You will have to give up your sensitivity. You ought to understand that I am not interested in passing judgment on you. If I say anything it is only for the sake of the analysis, and you ought not to worry what motives I have."

I said I brought up all these other matters because the time was short, and I had hoped to draw out some opinions on general questions from Freud.

"You wanted to impress me," said Freud.

"I don't think so," I said. "I was just curious to know how you approached a problem and tackled it."

"But that is not what an analysis is for," said Freud. "You are not here to get things out of me, wise words and the like; all that has nothing to do with the analysis."

"But it is tempting," I said, "because you are a great man, and I know how interesting Eckermann's conversations were"—an allusion to Eckermann's *Conversations with Goethe*.

I thought there was a brief approving silence at this point, but Freud said, "I am not acting differently from the way any other analyst would act in the same situation, no matter who he was."

I promised again to try to be good. "We shall see," said

Freud. "Some people make conscious promises, but with unconscious qualifications; we shall see."

"I'll do what I can," I said. I thereupon resumed the account of my difficult period a year and a half ago, and told of a girl I knew, a friend of my brother's, who developed an hysterical psychosis, which I tried unsuccessfully to treat; she had to go to a hospital for a while, where she recovered. Freud asked one or two questions in detail, and the hour ended.

"I will do what I can (*ich werde mein Möglichstes versuchen*)," I said again when I went out.

November 2, 1934

I started immediately with a recitation of three dreams: the first, of walking in the cold with my father; the second of the murder of a Negro woman servant by my landlady, the third, of a lecture in psychiatry by Professor Meyer. The third of these was the only one I could remember in some detail: Professor Meyer was older in the dream than he really was, and wore side whiskers. My wife was present with me, my friend Jack had come and I was pleased that he showed this interest in psychiatry. Though I had felt the scene of the dream was in Baltimore, actually it looked more like Boston. My interpretation of the dream was mainly that Professor Meyer (representing Freud?) wore bourgeois side whiskers because I had been thinking both he and Freud represented bourgeois psychology. Freud immediately interrupted to say the criticism was unjustified—that was the sort of thing the Communists said against him, but it was false.

"A science cannot be bourgeois," he said, "since it is only concerned with facts that are true everywhere."

"But," I said, "the facts are nothing but observations on patients, and these patients were largely from the middle classes."

"That is true," said Freud, "but that can't be helped; all the observations will hold true for a certain society. If the society changes, then the phenomena will be different."

Regarding the dream itself, I gave what associations I could about the scene and persons. I said that the patient whom Professor Meyer demonstrated wore glasses and looked like a certain obscure person who frequented the coffeehouse.

"It is of course possible that it is myself," I said, "though I do not think so."

"That is a well-known method of projection," said Freud, and evidently thought I had hit the nail on the head.

I went on in all honesty to give an account of my first visit to Meyer, and my attending doubts and feelings of inadequacy which disappeared when I met Meyer and talked to him. I also resumed my account of my feelings and thoughts then, and told of this or that friend whom I thought neurotic, including my wife—though I now felt I was mistaken.

"You see," said Freud, "that these recurrent compulsive ideas are related to your love-life." The hour ended here. I was not pleased to hear Freud's interpretation and said I admitted it only tentatively but with some reservations.

"You just mean you don't like it," said Freud.

November 5, 1934

Today's hour went rather smoothly and did not bring us far, for we were still concerned with settling old matters, and we got a bit involved in personalities. I said at the outset that I was feeling out of sorts—*verstimmt*.

"That is healthy," said Freud. I said that, considering what I had heard of myself up to now, I was not inclined to think much of myself.

"The judgment is premature," said Freud, "You should wait a while."

I had at least not known up to then that I was neurotic and that I had compulsory ideas.

"To the degree you have them," said Freud, "it is no great matter."

"At least," I said, "I didn't know I had these same troubles now, though I would be willing to talk about their significance in the past."

"All right then," said Freud. "It doesn't matter whether you have them now or not; the trouble can always come again. I had forewarned you at the outset that a neurosis can be revived in an analysis. But the interesting thing is how you turn everything into a judgment on you, as if that were the only thing that mattered."

"I don't like to lower my opinion of myself, without getting something in return," I said.

"That is not a scientific attitude," said Freud. "You have not yet completed the transition from the pleasure principle to the reality principle."

"That may be," I said, but I did not know what to answer. I proceeded with an account of some dreams, which did not appear relevant to our discussion, and revived various memories, but none of the dreams could actually be interpreted.

During a pause in my recitation, Freud said: "Say anything."

I said, "I am afraid I would launch off again into scientific discussion."

"But you see that is only a kind of *Widerstand*," said Freud. "You can say anything you like about me, too," he added.

"I don't know," I said. "I don't know which of us is the most sensitive."

"You know very well which of us is," said Freud, and he added, to avoid any misunderstanding, "It is you."

"Anyway," I said, "I don't usually like to fight."

At another point in the discussion, I said, "One hears a lot about emotional *Widerstand* to analysis, but less of an emotional *attraction* to the psychoanalytic procedure."

"That exists too," said Freud. "*Das gibt's auch.*"

"It seems to me," I said, "a great many things have occurred to me in your presence, and I have said a great many things, because I felt it would *accord* with your ideas or interests. I know you are interested in neurotic material. When I am with a friend who is interested in socialism, for an example, I think and talk socialism with him."

"But you ought not to care what I think," said Freud. Later he said that attitude of mine was so much *Widerstand*.

I paid Freud for the month and asked him if he would receipt the bill with the conventional German phrase, "*dankend solviert*"—"received with thanks"—so I could send it to America.

"Why with thanks?" he said. "I give you something which is at least as valuable as what you give me."

"I thought it was a mere technical formula," I said.

"Among businessmen, maybe," said Freud.

November 6, 1934
At this point I began to seriously question the whole conduct of the analysis, and felt mountains were being made

of molehills. I had thought of it in the afternoon, and decided that the clue to the whole past period that we had been discussing lay in the simple fact that during a time of loneliness and adversity I had felt discouraged and inadequate and had some self-depreciatory ideas which were dissipated when my situation was relieved. It was at this point that I determined that the best guarantee for the maintenance of healthy wholesome attitudes was the preservation of a way of life which was rich, meaningful, productive and thoroughly social. I felt that Freud's absorption with the subjective aspect of psychology was blinding him to the importance of real experience, of a person's way of life, of his social situation. It also began to become clear to me that the manner in which one conducted one's life could both relieve and induce psychological difficulties. I spoke to Freud of some of these ideas as I began to formulate them to myself, and added that under certain circumstances a degree of self-doubt and self-criticism seemed normal and healthy—it made one more human, increased one's sympathy and need not really interfere with work and happiness.

Freud thought this explanation of that past period sounded quite reasonable; it seemed to be a kind of successful compromise. He said there was in any case no special cause for concern, since all neurotic mechanisms occur in normal people, and there was no reason why I should picture myself as a severe neurotic.

I went on to say that I had Ellis to thank for the improvement of my spirits when I came to England. We experienced so much kindness and hospitality in England, and I had so much pleasure in my work, that I felt at home in the world again. Ellis was especially kind and considerate: one felt that he respected and valued one's individuality, and he himself seemed so much more shy than myself, with no apparent disadvantage, that I felt it was best to take myself for what I was, go about my business in my own way; perhaps shyness and some self-distrust were in the long run all to the good. One could not be everything at once: If I wanted to be a student of men and science, I need not be a charming and successful society figure too.

Freud said yes, Ellis was very kind and considerate, and that was why he was everywhere loved—"*seine allgemeine Beliebtheit.*"

"And he helps people too," I added.

"It's true that it is helpful to be liked by Ellis," said Freud, "but that is all superficial—it just gives you a kind of pleasant social standing. Ellis goes about and picks people, as one might pick out a good-looking woman at a ball. Naturally it is a satisfaction to a woman to be chosen in this way. But beauty is only skin deep. That kind of help doesn't go very far."

"But the feeling of sympathy one has is certainly very helpful," I protested. "It is like the positive transference of psychoanalysis, which is certainly an important part of the cure."

"No," said Freud. "I am glad you brought the question up, because I can clear up the misunderstanding: the positive transference is not part of the psychoanalytic therapy. The psychoanalytic cure consists in bringing unconscious material to consciousness; to this end the positive transference is used, but only as a means to an end, not for its own sake. It's the same with suggestions. It's true that the analyst uses suggestion, but only to help the psychoanalytic procedure."

Freud also began to talk of Ellis's relation to psychoanalysis. Ellis had some years ago written of psychoanalysis and said it made use of a procedure which was the opposite of scientific. If a patient admitted something, said Ellis, the analyst accepted it. If, however, the patient denied something, the analyst decided it was an admission too, concealed by a conscious denial. This, said Ellis, was like "heads I win, tails you lose." (Freud used the English phrase.)

"Now Ellis," said Freud, "was doing great harm to psychoanalysis by treating it so unjustly: it amounted to calling psychoanalysts a bunch of scoundrels (*Verbrecher*), and Ellis's opinions were likely to be influential."

Ellis did not know what he was talking about, Freud went on to say. It was no great matter if a man did not know anything about psychoanalysis, only he ought not to talk about it. At any rate, Ernest Jones, the London psychoanalyst, attacked Ellis—Freud thought it was in the *International Journal of Psychoanalysis*—and Ellis thereupon wrote to Freud in protest. Freud however felt it his duty to say, as politely as he could, that Jones was in the right. Freud told me this whole story, and I listened as sympathetically as I could, though I felt from my own experience that Ellis was not altogether wrong.

"Maybe he was three per cent right," I said. "An unskillful analyst could put together any kind of arbitrary theory on this basis."

"Of course," said Freud. "It all depends on the analyst. But we are sure he will use his judgment and experience. You always have to reckon on *Widerstand*. If there were no *Widerstand*, there would be no neuroses and no psychoanalysis, because nothing would ever have to be repressed."

I had brought along my Observations of a Psychiatric Interne, an account of my first assignment in a psychiatric hospital, which I thought Freud might want to read, but he politely declined, saying it was bad policy to use written material in an analysis. There was another reason, he added, but he would not tell me now.

I discussed a little essay of Freud's called *Die Verneinung* dealing with the significance of a patient's denials.

"It's true," said Freud, "that an analyst accepts an affirmation as such, because it means the patient consciously accepts the suggestion. If, however, the patient denies the suggestion it may either mean that it is true or untrue—that depends. The patient may simply not want to admit it. Generally, a patient simply neglects an inappropriate suggestion; if he reacts to it at all, it is generally a sign that there is something to it."

November 7, 1934

The hour went by with an empty recitation of activities and work interests. There were no dreams to report. It was as if I had tried all night, I said, and brought nothing to light for my pains.

November 8, 1934

I had several dreams during the night, both pleasant and unpleasant, and one sex dream, but felt refreshed and stimulated in the morning. My day was pleasant but busy, and I was obliged to come a little late to my hour. I started at once with a recitation of four dreams: one a simple sex dream, two of them concerned with hospital duties and my relations with the doctors, and the fourth, an anxiety dream, representing the death of a pregnant woman during an emergency operation. The symbolism in all these dreams was involved, and seemed to point to an interest in my shyness and in the hard lot of the poor. The dream of the death of a woman reminded me of unpleasant hospital experiences, but I could not associate the person with any specific woman. After a little thought, I said it could of course be my wife, but there was nothing in the dream to suggest it and I did not think so. Freud thereupon implied it was in all probability my wife, and said my denial simply strengthened the significance of the association.

In the dream, the doctor gave the poor patient a small sum of money—sixty-five groschen, or maybe three schillings, sixty-five groschen. Freud concentrated his attention on the numbers. "Numbers," he said, "are always significant." But I could get nothing out of them. Finally, he suggested that the number 365 reminded him of the days of the year. To this I responded that there were several things I associated with "year": I was concerned about how many years my present work would last; I also had thought that it would take years to patch up the neurosis Freud seemed to think I had. But I did not really think all this had anything to do with the dream.

At the end of the hour, Freud paid me a slight compliment by saying I had worked better in this hour than heretofore.

"I attribute that," I said with levity, "to revived gonadal activity."

"Possibly," he said.

November 9, 1934

Correspondence with Ellis continued, on various topics. In a letter dated November 6, 1934, he wrote, in response to an apparently cheerful letter of mine:

". . . it is satisfactory that you get on well with Freud, and succeed in keeping your end up, which must certainly be difficult with so dominating a person. . . ."

When I got to my analytic hour I told Freud that I dreamed that my landlord, who resembled Freud, found me prowling innocently about the house at night, and thereupon asked me to move out because I was a criminal. I thought the interpretation was simple: Freud had said a few days ago that it didn't matter to the analyst whether the patient was a saint or criminal. My own impression at that time was that the analyst in my case considered the patient more criminal than saintly, and I resented it. There was another person in the dream with whom I seemed to identify myself—an unpleasant but talented and ambitious young doctor, for whom nobody seemed to have a good word.

Freud seemed out of sorts during the hour and said little. I wondered if he even listened. He made only a few brief comments, and forgot occasional points. My stream of talk petered out. I went back to yesterday's dreams, which Freud asked me to repeat. I left the last one out—about the dying woman—and could not remember it. Freud reminded me, and added that my forgetting it showed it was repressed. He scored a point there, for it was certainly the least pleasant of the dreams.

I said I continued to feel well. I was pleasantly engaged in studying brain anatomy and was making good progress.

"Do you think you will find the cause of homosexuality that way?" asked Freud.

"No," I said, "but I have other interests besides that. Besides, it may give me hints. The pituitary gland at the base of the brain, for example, is certainly important in sex functions. I ought to know something about it. And there are other analogous neurological problems which may prove suggestive: left-handedness, for example—it may have the same kind of cause as homosexualtiy." Anyway, I continued, I also felt good because Professor Marburg had just started his little neuroanatomy seminar, and I found it very interesting. Moreover, I was happy over the turn the analysis had taken, and was glad that the little problem that we first discussed was cleared up.

"I am not so sure," said Freud.

"I at least hope so," I said, and thought to myself, it is not likely I will be befuddled into another maze of conflicting doubts soon again, not even at Freud's suggestion.

"Talking of denying things (*Verneinung*)," I said, "it occurred to me that I have denied a good many things already. I have for example already twice denied the possibly homosexual significance of two dreams I had." I repeated them. In one of them, I was simply walking with my father, in another I was talking to a London Bobby. I think I revived these denials with mischievous intent, and proceeded to talk of some homosexual acquaintances, and of my thoughts on homosexuality. Freud listened. I said I was glad I was not homosexual and felt perfectly satisfied with heterosexuality. It might be a consolation to think I could enjoy myself twice as much if I were bisexual, but it might also be true that I would have twice as many love troubles (*Liebeskummer*).

"But you haven't had any love troubles," said Freud, so that I reminded him of some that I had had.

I was glad, I said, that Freud was more pleased with my "work," though I said it was more like play.

"I simply meant," said Freud, "that you were cooperating more, and not criticizing so much. Next week again," he concluded. We shook hands, and he said, "*Adieu*."

I was unfortunately (and really unavoidably) late again. "That means *Widerstand*," said Freud, and I was at pains to explain that it was really unavoidable. Freud was, I think, not altogether convinced.

I remarked that parts of the last letter from Ellis saddened me, for he spoke of his failing energies. "When one is old," said Freud, "what can one expect?"

"It is a sad world," I said, "everything is topsy-turvy and rotten; all that Ellis stands for is forgotten, and war may come now any minute. What has a young man to look forward to? What chance has he to feel he can do useful work against the background of this huge rottenness—this *Scheusslichkeit*?"

"I am sorry I can say nothing against that," said Freud, "for I share your opinion. People like Ellis have little power now."

I spoke of various things in my past—my feelings about being a Jew, my views on anti-Semitism, and my not infrequent thoughts about death. "That is quite common in young people," said Freud. With reference to the Jewish question, he agreed that Jews were forced into closer relations to each other by pressure from the outside.

"In England, France and Italy especially," he said, "where the Jews are freely recognized, they are all strongly patriotic."

I had occasion to mention an article Ellis once wrote against anti-Semitism, in which Freud's name was mentioned with high praise, and Freud again seemed pleased. I spoke of my great liking for England. "I can understand that," said Freud. "I have always been a strong Anglo-

phile." He said his son was now in London. I had heard of
him through Ellis. I said it was only in England that one
could find so many high-minded people in so small a space,
and Freud agreed. We came to speak again of the frequency
of homosexuality in England, and Freud again said he felt it
was particularly common there—and in Germany too. Ellis
had denied this. Freud said it was particularly pronounced
among the leaders of English thought . . . among writers
and the like. I did not know if he was right. He said it was
merely his impression.

I told Freud of Professor Pötzl's lecture last night on
"Brain and Mind (*Gehirn und Seele*)," an ambitious subject, and Freud was interested to hear what Pötzl said. He
was pleased to hear that his name was prominently mentioned. "Pötzl, you know, was a pupil of mine," he said, "but
he has since gone his own way."

There was not much more to say. Freud told me to speak
of anything. "Just let your mind drift," he said in English.
"You don't have to speak of things that happen now," he
added. "Anything will do, past or present, since it is all of
one piece, and our purpose is to see the structure of your
mind, like an anatomist."

I spoke of various little things, such as peculiarities
I thought I had. I said for example that I sometimes ab-
sent-mindedly scratched my head or cleaned my nails.

"You ought to break yourself of the habit," said Freud.

Of my dreams, I could remember nothing, though I
thought I must have had some. But I had followed Freud's
advice and made no effort to remember. At the end of the
hour, Freud rose quietly as usual, and I followed.

The fiftieth anniversary of Koller's discovery of the effect of cocaine on the eye was celebrated recently, and I spoke to Freud about it and of his share in the discovery.

"There is not the least question who deserves the credit for it," he said, implying it was Koller. *"Es ist eine klare Sache*—it is a clear matter."

I said it almost always happens that a discovery is in the air at any given time and several people can be found working on the same task.

"Not always," he said. "Roentgen rays, for example, were discovered by a single worker."

"I understand, however, that was largely an accident," I said.

"But there is an element of chance in every discovery," said Freud.

"Well," I said, to get back to myself, "I am not myself working on any great discovery now; it is not likely that I shall ever make one."

"Do you think it necessary then?" asked Freud.

"No," I said, "but some great idea would help me to concentrate my work and interests; at present everything interests me and I get nowhere, just acquire a smattering of every subject. In medicine you have to work intensely in a small field. It is too vast an area to cover nowadays, and I have too many distracting interests. I console myself with the idea that there is still a place for somebody to attempt to coordinate knowledge in different fields, even if his knowledge has to remain superficial."

I related a few dreams I had; one of them was a thought rather than a dream in which I seemed worried at the possibility that my analysis would turn up a neurosis; there was another dream in which I spoke Italian to a little girl in the presence of Professor Bauer and his wife, but this produced no very significant associations. I had seen the wife and liked her, and the girl corresponded to a picture of a little girl I had seen in the paper. Bauer had recently spoken Italian to a patient. Freud suggested that the dream meant I preferred Bauer's wife to him, and that there was an identification or comparison of myself with Bauer.

November 14, 1934

"Does a didactic analysis differ from an ordinary analysis in any important respect?" I asked.

"Not essentially," said Freud; "only insofar as the material and progress of the analysis is different. With a neurotic patient the analysis must follow the fluctuations of symptoms and *Widerstand* and adapts itself to the state of the patient at any given time. With a healthy student, these fluctuations don't always occur unless he is neurotic to start with or becomes neurotic during the analysis. I have been waiting for this question, for I knew that you would pretty soon ask where we were getting, and I must admit that from an analytic point of view we are not getting far. You are a so-called normal person—*Sie gehören den sogenannten Gesunden an.* You have found your contentment by the same processes that occur in psychoanalysis, by consolidation [I am not sure I understood this] and adjustment. You can be sure you have your repressions (*Verdrängungen*), too, only they don't show themselves. You have no incentive for showing them. The only reason you can have for cooperating in an analysis is scientific curiosity. You notice my methods with you have changed. I tried to use personal criticism for a while, but you were too sensitive to it, and began to criticize me in turn, so that I have had to treat you more carefully (*schonend*) lately." I was pleased to hear that Freud thought me so sound, and I said I was not so sure I was so well-adjusted and contented.

"It's true," I said, "I go about my business and when frustrated do the next best thing, on principle, but this full activity does not mean that I have no problems inside. There are many times when I am sad, sometimes for long periods."

"Everybody has such periods," said Freud.

"Lately, however," I said, "it is true I have been feeling well and contented although I've had my doubts and apprehensions."

"Your subjective sense of well-being can be objectively confirmed," said Freud, "for I have the same impression."

"There are probably people in my circle of acquaintances though," I said, "who would be less sure of my thorough soundness, and I have from time to time heard unpleasant things about myself."

"Why?" asked Freud.

"I don't always have a free and easy manner with people. I get terribly self-conscious sometimes, especially with certain people." I elaborated, "Maybe it is a guilty conscience—*Schuldgefühl*," and apologized for using a technical expression.

"Why?" said Freud.

"Well," I said, "I do lots of things which don't accord with the standards or values of my community, and I feel they would disapprove." I said, for example, I often felt self-conscious in the presence of Ellis, not however before Freud.

"But Ellis is certainly not a conventional person," said Freud. "He would not consider you immoral."

"I don't know," I said. "I act so meanly sometimes that I

wonder what Ellis would think of me if he could know. Besides, I feel Ellis may have too high an opinion of me, and I am undeserving." I reminded Freud of his little essay *Die am Erfolge scheitern*, and said I might be an example of those who take successes badly. I always seem to find myself too much admired and too seldom liked; at least I was often troubled by that idea, though it probably was not strictly true. I used to think I had too many successes and a few failures here and there might make me more human.

"Still, you do not seem to like my disparaging remarks— quite the contrary."

"Everything in moderation," I said. "When a young man hears he is not suited to the profession to which he will probably dedicate his life, it is rather disconcerting."

"I didn't say you were not suited to it," said Freud. "I had simply said 'no extraordinary talent.' "

"It wasn't so much the criticism anyway," I said; "it was the manner in which it was said."

At any rate, the atmosphere was advantageous for a recital of all my little difficulties with this or that person, social shyness, wanting to be better liked, etc. Freud listened attentively. I again revived the recollections of a year ago, and tried to give them the moderate emphasis they deserved, which was something less than they were accorded up to now in the analysis. At that time I was perfectly able to go about my work with ease and tolerable contentment, and even had very good times occasionally. The whole episode did not last, even then, more than two months or so.

"A person can have ideas like that once or twice," said Freud, "but there is no reason why he should think he is being put in the same class as a severe neurotic. That shows your tendency to think in abstractions again. I refer to the ideas as compulsive and immediately you take the big jump to the conclusion that you are classed as a neurotic."

At this point Freud's big chow was heard scratching on the door, and Freud rose, as he often had before, to let the dog in. She settled on the carpet and began licking her private parts. Freud did not approve of this behavior, and tried to make her stop. "It's just like psychoanalysis," he said.

I asked whether any of the psychoanalytic theories could be proved by animal experimentation. One could, for example, easily find out whether a monogamous ape chooses its mother-type in picking a partner.

"That is not psychoanalysis," said Freud, "though psychoanalysis can make use of such knowledge."

We spoke of myself; I described further examples of shyness, but said I was not much troubled by it, and gave my own explanation, which, right or wrong, had satisfied me up to now.

"All that sounds plausible and reasonable," said Freud, "but we can only discover what it really means by studying your dreams. We have to see the other side of the picture."

November 15, 1934

Unfortunately the clock at the Neurological Institute was a few minutes slow and I came late again. I tried to explain but psychoanalytic theory was against me and it was clear that Freud again considered it so much *Widerstand*. "Work well now to make up for it," he said, but he was in an irritable mood throughout the hour, and kept tapping on the sofa-head with his fingertips. I went straight to business with the best of intentions, and added a detail to my dream about Bauer the day before: that I did not know whether to look him in the eyes or not, a thought that frequently occurred to me in waking life. I then went on to describe a further dream: a man resembling Buffalo Bill and his wife had a daughter whom I examined psychiatrically. Perhaps I found something—I didn't know—but I noticed that the father was particularly irritable and on close examination, he turned out to have an incipient general paresis.

Regarding the dream, I said I had just the day before made a diagnosis of general paresis at the Bauer clinic on a case that had been overlooked.

I made the further interpretation: I was the father, general paresis was an abnormality, and my own irritability sometimes seemed abnormally intense. The daughter might be T.O. or my wife, the wife might be my wife—I wasn't sure. I told a little of T.O. and her mother; Freud had me spell the name. Furthermore, I had a little conversation with my wife the night before which seemed pertinent. I had told her that Freud said I was healthy, but I added jokingly that I had swindled him really and I was in fact crazy as a loon.

Freud thereupon said he did not mean to flatter me by calling me healthy. I was just one of those supposedly healthy (*angeblich gesunden*) people who went about without much trouble because their complexities were stored away out of reach.

"There is no reason to feel proud of it," he said.

"One likes to be healthy," I said, "but I was not altogether sure you did me justice. I don't like those smooth people who seem to have no troubles. They don't attract my sympathy and aren't very likeable."

"It's enviable, to be sure," said Freud, "but it doesn't mean anything. But when I said you had a tendency to ruminate you didn't like the idea and rejected it right away."

"In fact," I said, "it bothered me because I thought it might be true. But ruminations or obsessions are ideas that come again and again to consciousness—"

"That's right," said Freud.

"—and I had no such idea," I continued. "It was simply a fact that I had no such idea. In spite of the strong stimulus the analysis gave, I found I was not concerned with any of my old preoccupations. It is true I had one preoccupation for a while, but it was only for a short time, and never previously or since. Lots of people have had that kind of idea. It depends on the extent and intensity," I said.

"Exactly," said Freud; "but it doesn't matter what I say, you always disagree."

"I don't disagree," I said. "I simply examine everything you say critically. I see that people are fooled by their prejudices: they like to believe what is pleasant and deny what is unpleasant. It was pleasant to be called healthy, but I was not so sure it was correct. At least, I considered the question. Is that kind of healthiness desirable then?" I asked myself. "Is it something to be aimed at?"

"Certainly," said Freud, but he was not clear.

"I certainly have my share of troubles," I said, and went on to tell him of all my troubles again: not feeling at ease with some people, or thinking I was not accepted; my continual feeling that people around me had outlooks different from mine. "So that even among friends," I added, "I don't always feel at home. Maybe I make enemies because I feel at home among them," I said, attempting a deeper analysis. "I don't know. Sometimes I think I may antagonize people on purpose. Maybe I like to fight too much." I talked on and on in this way, and seemed to reach low depths. Afterwards I felt I had drawn a much less favorable picture of my relations to my group than I deserved. Freud made little comment. I felt baffled again.

At the end of the hour I shook hands with him. "I hope I develop a neurosis," I said in all sincerity, meaning, I suppose, that some interesting neurotic material would emerge.

"Tomorrow again," he said.

November 16, 1934

I described a few dreams with transparent sexual motives, and there was a little pause thereafter. I had the weary feeling, I said, that the analysis was not progressing through some fault of mine, and I sometimes felt confused. Freud said: "You are quite right. The analysis is not progressing. I don't know why. Nothing has turned up: everything is so simple. I propose that we try it for another two weeks, let's say, and if it is still going badly, let us give it up, and you can save the money."

"I don't know why that should be so," I said. "I am perfectly willing to learn, and I am willing to give everything a hearing, even unpleasant things about myself. It is certainly strange that a scientist should not be allowed access to a body of knowledge because he happens not to have personal problems; I know I have a sincere wish to learn something about psychoanalysis."

"But psychoanalysis is different from other sciences," said Freud; "there is no other science where the unconscious is so important."

"Perhaps something will turn up in time," I said. "You say I am supposedly healthy; are there any really healthy people then?"

"Healthiness is a purely conventional practical concept,"

he said, "and has no real scientific meaning. It simply means that a person gets on well: it doesn't mean that the person is particularly worthy. There are 'healthy' people who are not worth anything, and on the other hand 'unhealthy' neurotic people who are very worthy (*wertvoll*) individuals indeed."

"Does this 'healthiness' correspond to the state of a person after a successful analysis?" I asked.

"It does in a way," he said. "Analysis enriches the individual but he loses some of his Ego, his *Ich*. It may not always be worth while." (I am not sure I have recorded this last statement correctly.)

I said it was strange that nothing had come out of my analysis so far. Didn't my dreams indicate anything?

"They are all so simple," said Freud; "they don't reveal anything."

"Perhaps I have a simple unconscious," I suggested. "You must realize that I and my friends were brought up partly under your influence and I may have less reason to repress things than some of your other patients."

"It's quite possible," said Freud. "At any rate, up to now I have not been able to tell you anything you didn't know yourself." He here quoted Shakespeare to the effect: "to hear something you already know will never make you wise"— or something similar. I did not recognize the quotation.†

"But there were other problems that did not seem so clear to me," I said. "My self-consciousness, for example."

"That is no great matter," said Freud. "Perhaps it simply means that you would like people to have a good opinion of you. As you yourself say, it is perfectly natural and usual."

† Possibly Mark Antony's:

> I only speak right on;
> I tell you that which you yourselves do know.
>> Julius Caesar III, 2, 228.

Freud seemed in a kindly and rather self-effacing mood. We came around to discuss some general topics. "Psychoanalysis has had such a wide influence, it is perfectly natural that I should want to learn more of it," I said.

"I am not so sure of its influence," said Freud. "You probably are referring to its emphasis on sex."

"Not only that," I said. "The idea of the unconscious too."

"That doesn't seem to have made much progress in psychology," said Freud. I spoke a little more in praise of psychoanalysis, but Freud reminded me that at the beginning of the analysis I seemed to think differently of it.

"But that was just so much discussion," I said. "I don't know enough to actually criticize it yet."

"That may be so," said Freud. "I tried to change your attitude by criticizing you, but you defended yourself and probably were right to do so. At any rate, that doesn't seem to be helping your analysis," he said, returning to our theme.

I believe he said that I had "character resistance" (*Charakterwiderstände*). That was something new to me, and carried slightly unpleasant connotations. "I hope we shall be able to go on," I said.

"We shall see how it goes," said Freud.

November 19, 1934

Another off day. Very little progress was made, but there was considerable talk just the same. I said I had moods of self-reproach for being so resistant a subject during analysis. "Character resistance" suggested something undesirable to me, and I was sorry I was so difficult. It is true, Freud replied, that I was critical of myself and thought frequently of myself, as an intelligent conscientious person should do, but it was all superficial; in my unconscious I was proud and complacent, and resistant to the analytic procedure in spite of my avowed respect for Freud. "A person is made up of several parts," he explained: in some respects I felt inferior perhaps, but not in others, and my professions of respect were just the familiar counterpart (*bekannte Gegenstück*) to my real feelings. Freud again began to speak with vehemence, and I could again think of nothing better to say than that I was very sorry I seemed so proud; I did not want to be, I recognized it was unpleasant, and it might later make for unhappiness. It would certainly be worth-while and helpful, I added, to find the cause of this peculiarity and remove it. I felt depressed and discouraged again when I left.

November 21, 1934

Freud's unusually friendly tone continued. I had a rather complete and fantastic dream involving my wife and a fish chopping machine. "That's what I call a real dream," said Freud with zest and proceeded to an interpretation. He thought it related to my feelings toward analysis: the fish, meaning me, were being put, so to speak, through the works. The fish was a well-known symbol for the penis; it remained to be explained though why I was represented by so many male organs. For the rest of the hour Freud explained the nature of psychoanalytic symbols, following the line of his lecture on that subject in his introductory *Vorlesungen*. He also answered my questions which, he said, I was fully entitled to ask (*vollauf berechtigt*). The meaning of the symbols was found from a study of folklore, philology, dreams and neuroses. The use of symbols in dreams was not a direct form of dream distortion, and was not necessarily the work of the dream censor.

"Many dream symbols are inborn and innate," he went on;

"they arise spontaneously as a child learns to talk, and many children's neuroses are readily explained by a reference to their symbolic meaning."

"Why," I asked, "do I sometimes dream of the real thing and sometimes of the symbol?"

Freud had no answer for this. "It cannot be explained," he said. "It just happens." The dream, he said, very often meant exactly the opposite of what it seemed to say; not only that: if the dream were told backwards, it often reveals its secrets.

"How does one know if the dream is correctly interpreted?" I asked. "From the response of the patient?"

"All interpretations are tentative," said Freud. "One cannot work from a single dream; one must have a series of them, and fill them into the general scheme." He led me into his adjoining study to show me a sample of an old phallic bird symbol from his fine collection of ancient bronze miniatures and figurines.

"You see now," he said later, "why it was that I disapproved of your having prejudices concerning dream interpretations. Not only ought one not to have preconceived ideas, but you were too young and inexperienced to venture any ideas on that subject at all."

I thanked Freud for his pains, and the stimulating account he had given, and left in some distress, because I did not believe in this psychoanalytic theory of dream symbols. Although I recognized the partial truth of many of Freud's observations it still seemed to me that he neglected the fact that the thinking process in dreams was basically affected by the *inefficiency* of mental functions under the conditions of sleep.

My mild moodiness continued; I felt physically in poor tone and my mood threw a little shadow over everything. I did the best I could in analysis and spoke valiantly onwards to no great purpose, and Freud said very little. I spoke much of my young radical friends, and the reception they gave me when I first returned to America. I was soon made to feel that I was outside their group. "Ah, youth!" exclaimed Freud, when the hour ended.

I ventured to tell Freud today that his view of the inborn innate character of dream symbols did not agree with my notions of inheritance: I did not know whether one could inherit such abstract ideas, especially since they were bound up with language, which is an acquired activity: it implied the inheritance of acquired characteristics.

"Of course," said Freud. "If one didn't believe in inheritance, there would be a lot we could not explain; all of evolution would be impossible." I pointed out that there were other possible ways of explaining evolution, that Darwin himself did not attach great importance to Lamarckism and that most biologists were sceptical of it.

"But we can't bother with the biologists," he said. "We have our own science. (*Wir können uns um die Biologen nicht kümmern. Wir haben unsere eigene Wissenschaft.*)"

"But any science ought not to be inconsistent with another," I said.

"We must go our own way," said Freud.

"Maybe biologists will come to believe in Lamarckism,"

I said. "J. B. S. Haldane admitted to me that it was possible."
"There, you see," said Freud—"*Da sehen Sie.*"

November 27, 1934

I dreamed that I was in the gallery of a theatre and watched a man in military costume doing tricks with a sword. I looked down into the orchestra, thought of the danger of a fall, grew frightened and called to my wife for help. I awakened. Toward an interpretation, I could only suggest that I had been reading in the paper of the danger of war, and that a new military patriotic play was to open in a few days and was being widely advertised.

Freud gave me a systematic explanation, but said that at the present stage of the analysis he did not expect that I would accept it: Sitting in a theatre always meant watching coitus; children often see something of the sort and associate it, perhaps rightly, with something frightening or with an act of aggression: hence the military aspect. The drawing of a sword from its sheath was a symbol for the sex act, even though the sword was being withdrawn, since dreams often showed the opposite of what they mean. Falling is a constant symbol for femininity, for giving birth or being born. Hence in Austria, *niederkommen* and in France *accoucher* meant to give birth; one also spoke of a *Wurf* or a litter of animals. Freud also quoted the Homeric Greek phrase for giving birth or being born: "falling between the woman's legs," I think it was. The dream meant I was watching coitus, was identifying myself with the female part and was disturbed by the feminine elements in myself.

"No," he said in answer to a question, 'the dream is not homosexual. If you were homosexual, you would not be disturbed by your femininity: it is a type of dream that occurs more often among men than among women and more often among heterosexual than homosexual men; every man has some feminine elements in his nature." I decided afterwards to ask Freud whether this statement had been, or could be, statistically demonstrated. Furthermore I did not believe I had ever witnessed human coitus.

November 28, 1934

I suggested to Freud that his views on falling dreams might easily be confirmed by statistics. "That is a typical American idea," he said. "You can't study psychology with statistics. Falling has other meanings besides femininity; it may mean giving birth." He was apparently displeased with the suggestion, and though I said another word or two in its defense, I soon changed the subject.

November 29, 1934

My wife had spoken in her sleep with reference, I thought, to some friend of hers whom I did not like. Freud said talking in one's sleep came from a wish to communicate something, and my wife *wished* to annoy me. But I knew that she sometimes talked when she slept alone, and awakened herself. Freud could not explain this, but simply said talking in one's sleep was not a common phenomenon.

I had a dream in which I felt I was going to die from a cancer of my face, and interpreted it in accordance with what I supposed was psychoanalytic theory, by saying that I was feeling injured by the analytic procedure, but Freud thought it meant that I wished he would die from his cancer (for which he had actually already undergone several operations) because of the unpleasant things he said.

November 30, 1934

I continued to feel blue. Ellis had written a friendly card to me, and mentioned that the poetess H.D. was in town and that I ought to meet her. Freud knew her address, but I was in no mood to meet strangers; I was usually too shy, I told Freud.

"You should break yourself of that," he said.

"Ellis," I said, "would say I ought rather to do as I liked."

"That is another method, too," said Freud. For the rest, he said everybody has his ups and downs.

I spoke of a few points in neurology that had come up during my day's work, concerning the function of the frontal lobes, but Freud made no comment. I revived the subject of homosexuality, and Freud spoke of his own views: everybody had a homosexual component in his nature; most social feeling was nothing but sublimated homosexuality.

"Do you mean that socially good people like Einstein and Romain Rolland are doing nothing but sublimating their homosexuality?"

"Exactly," said Freud. He was at some pains to explain that psychoanalysis was the only school of psychology which claimed the universality of homosexual tendencies.

I commented that Otto Weininger (in 1903, I think) brought out the idea in his *Geschlecht und Charakter*.

"He was a friend of mine," said Freud, "but he got the idea from analysis and used it in an improper way."

"It would be interesting to know why the feeling against homosexuality is so universal in our time," I asked.

"It was always so," said Freud, "even in ancient Greece. People repress their own homosexuality and if the repression is strong enough, they adopt a hostile attitude."

December 4, 1934

We chatted pleasantly on a variety of minor matters today, of an interesting case I had seen, of the status of psychoanalysis in America, etc. I had two or three dreams to tell of, but nothing new came out. Freud was extremely pleasant and the atmosphere was friendly.—Concerning dreams, I asked whether eight hours of successive dreaming can all be interpreted according to psychoanalytic theory; the assumption so often seemed to be made that a dream was a neatly rounded little entity.

"Why not?" he said. "Dreaming is nothing but a continuation of waking thought."

December 5, 1934

I again had a dream in which the subject of homosexuality was discussed, but it pointed in no direction, and Freud said all one could guess was that the subject was engaging my attention. It was, and I asked some questions about it. If social feeling is so often sublimated homosexuality, then active homosexualists ought to have less social feeling since they sublimate less—but this was not the case.

This form of argument did not appeal to Freud, but he answered patiently that there were all sorts of degrees and types, and no rule held for all. I then proceeded to another theoretical question: why did not one say simply that *all* mental activity was directed toward wish-fulfillment, why just simply dreams?

Freud did not like this theoretical expansion at all, and said dreams were different *essentially*, and not only quantitatively, from waking thoughts. He admitted there were transitional states between dream and waking life but said the rules only hold for dreams, and dreams only occurred in sleep. "Twilight states or delirium have different laws," he said. He then proceeded to criticize me roundly again for launching out into abstractions, though I defended myself with some confidence, for I did not believe that dreams are essentially different from other mental activity.

"You ought to listen and learn," he said. "You have been receptive to Ellis, now you ought to learn something from me. I can't make a psychoanalyst of you in this short time, but I can give you the stimulus in that direction."

I soon changed the subject. Perhaps I was simply one of those ineffectual theorizers, I said, that Ramon y Cajal, the neuroanatomist, had spoken of in a recent book.

"He is dead, isn't he?" said Freud.

He had just died. Freud went into his study to find out how old he had been; he was eighty-two. Freud was then seventy-eight. Freud spoke of him and his predecessor, Golgi. Obersteiner, the famous Viennese neurologist, whom Freud knew, had once demonstrated some old specimens of Golgi's and spoken condescendingly of them.

"Golgi was neglected all his life," said Freud, "though he is a recognized name in medical history now." The old hopes of the neurological anatomists, he added, were never realized.

"Psychology and physiology are now coming into their own," I said. I spoke of an interesting case of hysteria-like convulsions in a hypoglycemic patient I had seen.

"The relation between the physical and mental states: that is a field for work in the future!" he said with enthusiasm.

December 6, 1934

I had seen an article in an American magazine which quoted an answer of Freud's to a question on war. But

Freud had never answered such a question, and the article was evidently faked or stolen from his writings.

"That sort of thing happens in America," I said.

"It happens often enough here," said Freud.

I had one or two dreams of simple content: one praising myself and my future, another wishing that I could be alone for a while—both interpreted according to psychoanalytic theory. We discussed a little incident where I had occasion to show jealousy, and Freud suggested the possibility of an unconscious homosexual jealousy mechanism, such as he had elaborated in his writings.

"Possibly," I said, but I saw no reason to assume it. Regarding homosexuality as a whole, I quoted Wilhelm Busch:

> *Schön ist's vielleicht anderswo*
> *Doch hier sind wir sowieso.*
> (It might be nice some other place
> But here we are in any case.)

I felt quite satisfied with heterosexuality. I couldn't be otherwise, I added, because those were my habits. "That is not the only reason," said Freud. "If you attempted to act homosexual, you would find that you had internal psychic resistance to it too. You may be able to make a homosexual person bisexual in behavior by releasing his heterosexual component, but you cannot so easily make a heterosexual person bisexual in the same way, for the resistance is much greater, and the inducements far fewer."

"What, by the way, is the cause of heterosexuality?" I asked.

Freud gave a brief resumé of the psychoanalytic theories of the question of object choice (*Objektwahl*), and I listened attentively. The choice of a male or female as sex partner developed in accordance with the castration complex, and it all involved early family experiences.

"But suppose a child has no family," I suggested; "suppose the mother dies at childbirth and the father brings up the boy; what happens, then?"

"The boy would then usually become homosexual," said Freud.

"It would be interesting to investigate such cases," I said.

"It is not necessary," said Freud. "We know how they work out without that." Freud again showed he was not sympathetic to this kind of approach, and he was again growing irritated.

"If one can assume the inheritance of dream symbols," I said, "why not assume that a heterosexual impulse can be inherited?"

"It simply doesn't work that way," said Freud.

"Are human beings different from animals in that respect?" I asked.

"In many respects they are," said Freud, "but the animals rather prove this point: all they are interested in is genital satisfaction, and it is simply the convenience of the opposite sex for that end that makes them heterosexual."

I could not follow all this argument in its details, but I supposed it was all clearly explained in his writings. Freud was not too pleased with my discussion. He mentioned Ellis several times, only to praise him for his caution and respect for facts.

"Ellis once told me," I said, "that the older he got the less sure he grew of everything. I am curious to know if you have had the same feeling."

"I am older than Ellis," said Freud with emphasis, "and

I can say that the older I get the more sure I grow of everything. I have had the friendliest relations—by letter—with Ellis for over thirty-five years, but I have always criticized him for having made too few decisions (*Er macht zu wenig Urteile*). And now in his old age it is no wonder that he feels uncertain. You have the same fault, and you gave yourself away at the beginning of the analysis, by saying you were satisfied to be shrouded in the luminous mist of truth, or something like that."

"That," I said, "was a quotation from Goethe."

"Well, Goethe had that same fault, and that is the reason why a number of his scientific writings have lost their value for us."

"One can't be everything," I said. "I hope something worth-while is left in me."

"Yes," said Freud, "but you ought to know your faults. I have my own faults, but nobody can say that I have been lax in self-criticism. In this or that detail I've had to change my views, and some things which I thought were completely true turned out to be partial truths but in essentials I have had no reason to change my conclusions. Ellis years ago said that we put too much emphasis on early sexual trauma, and he was right; now we are more cautious. We also recognize the importance of constitutional factors, but what they are we don't know, whereas we know the psychological mechanisms. School-boys in England, for example, have, most of them, homosexual experiences, but they usually get over them—there must be other factors involved."

When I spoke of the wish fulfillment theory of dreams, Freud said that distortion (*Entstellung*) was a more regular and certain characteristic of dreams than the wish fulfillment (*Wunscherfüllung*). Freud then remarked that constitutional factors and effeminacy were less striking in male than their counterparts in female homosexuals, for the latter were especially likely to have masculine mannerisms and attire.

When I sounded Freud out on the relative importance of constitution and of psychogenesis in the development of homosexuality he sidestepped the question by saying they were inextricably linked together. (*Man kann sie nicht auseinander halten.*)

The hour ended here, and I left.

December 7, 1934

I praised Freud's chapter on infantile sexuality in his introductory *Vorlesungen* and said it was strange to read slighting remarks on him immediately afterwards in Bing's textbook of neurology.

"Who is Bing?" asked Freud with interest, for he had never heard of him.

"It is curious," I said: "strictly neurological work and psychological insight are so very different, it was rare to find a talent for both in the same man."

"It is not necessary," said Freud. "Psychology and neurology are two separate things."

"But it is very important to be able to distinguish between organic and psychic disease."

"Yes," he said, "it is important for diagnosis, and not thereafter."

"How can a mere psychologist make the diagnosis then, if he does not know neurology?" I asked, and gave some examples of mistakes of this kind I had seen.

"After a week of analysis you can usually decide," said Freud.

I reminded Freud of an early French essay of his on the relative importance of heredity in the neuroses, and was anxious to get his present view on that subject. He was extremely evasive.

"One can't express it in percentages," he said, and chided me again for launching into theory.

"But this is an eminently practical matter," I insisted. "Everybody is talking of eugenics and heredity and the opinion of a person of your experience is important. Bauer, for example, always puts strong emphasis on heredity in psychopathic states."

"If he has studied the matter, he ought to know," said Freud.

"You often speak of constitutional factors," I said. "Do you mean inherited or acquired organic conditions?"

"Both," he said. "By constitutional I mean everything that is not psychological." By this time it was obvious that Freud's interest was in psychoanalysis, not eugenics, and I resumed my account of myself.

December 10, 1934

Nothing of great importance in today's hour. We chatted for a few minutes about some mutual acquaintances. Freud spoke highly of Schilder. I related a simple sexual dream in which a girl engaged in some intimacies with me, and made the perhaps mischievous, though psychoanalytically proper, attempt to interpret it homosexually. Freud did not admit the interpretation, and his contradiction came so promptly and easily that I felt the surest way to coax him to say something was to say the opposite. I thought there was more than a streak of negativism in Freud, as there was more than a streak of pessimism, and I began to believe this personal quality had found expression in psychoanalytic theory.

A second dream, about traveling in a lift, I also attempted to interpret homosexually, and Freud again said the opposite: it was a dream about birth, he said, an Oedipus dream. So it was, for later in the dream my mother appeared, and there was a tender passage. There was some eating in this dream too, and eating, said Freud, was a natural symbol for one's mother. One of my associations went back to the same Schilder we had just discussed.

"But that," I said, "was probably a mere coincidence, because we were just talking about Schilder."

"In analysis," said Freud, "one admits coincidences as little as possible." There was no doubt that psychoanalysis proceeded on this principle; it was the denial of the possibility of coincidence which led Freud to think favorably of mental telepathy.

My mood at this time began to be a combination of scientific bewilderment, because I could not accept many of Freud's conclusions and was essentially out of sympathy with his attitude, and personal displeasure, for I did not like the idea of being constantly probed for morbid features of my psychology.

December 11, 1934

I recited a few recent dreams to Freud, the only one of consequence being the following: I walk along the street and a detective tells me to stop. I walk on heedless. He threatens to shoot if I do not stop. I go on, and feel a shot in my shoulder. I bind it with a tourniquet and awaken soon after.

The detective reminded me of one from the Missing Persons Bureau in New York whom I had seen in Bellevue Psychiatric Hospital checking on patients who had attempted suicide. He used to get irritated when a moribund patient would be unable to give him the information he wanted. My interpretation was: I am threatened, and told unpleasant things during analysis, but I don't care and go my own way.

Freud grew indignant: "An attitude of that sort makes further analysis impossible: it is purely emotional."

"Naturally," I said, "it is emotional; rationally nothing ought to bother me. I don't see why that need interfere with the analysis."

"What about the wound and the bandage? Why were you shot in the shoulder?"

"I had to be shot somewhere; why not in the shoulder?" I said. "Perhaps I was lying on my shoulder, or had my hand on my wife's shoulder during sleep, as I often do. I don't know if that is significant."

"Everything is," said Freud.

"Maybe," I said, "but if I begin to associate with all the infinite other things in the dream: the street I was on, the clothes I wore etc., I might put emphasis on the wrong spot."

Freud was irritated. "But you didn't mention these other things." As a matter of fact I did mention that it took place near my house. "We have to follow up the things you mention; the second part of the dream is still unexplained, but you can go on with other things, if you like." I picked up the discussion of homosexuality. I said that his statement that he found all his subjects in analysis more or less bisexual was a great revelation to me, if it was true, and I was assuming it was. For people like myself, who generally did not see the necessity for repressing their impulses, it ought to follow that we ought to become bisexual in our activities; indeed it might seem desirable to urge reform in that direction.

Freud disagreed: "It would make life too complex," he said. "It would be impractical. You cannot give your impulses free hand. You have to keep them in control, not repress them; keeping oneself in control does not lead to neuroses, at worst merely to discontent."

"But why control an impulse that does nobody any harm, and which leads to a purely private relation between two parties?"

"It would never do," said Freud. "How could you preserve discipline in an army, for example, if the officers kept falling in love with the soldiers and with each other?"

"But is there any scientific justification for interfering with such private affairs?" I asked. I mentioned that in Russia, for example, the laws against homosexuality were being revived. I did not know why, but I supposed that homosexuality began to increase when it was openly tolerated.

"No doubt," said Freud.

"But is there any scientific justification for such laws?" I asked.

"Science has nothing to do with laws," said Freud. "They are purely practical expedients. Homosexuality was found to be undesirable."

"The same argument about the difficulty of discipline is applied against coeducation in the schools in America," I said.

"But in children it is not so important, up to the age of twelve or thirteen their sexuality is only latent and does not produce such complications."

"But how about coeducation in colleges?" I asked.

"There you see all the complex results," said Freud. "The young men fall in love with the young girls and often marry them, and in America the girls are usually much more mature than the men at that early age, lead them around by the nose, make fools of them, and that is why you get your *Frauenherrschaft*, your rule of women, in America. That is one main reason why you have the sort of culture you have in America, and so many other things. American women are an anticultural phenomenon (*eine kulturwidrige Erscheinung*). They have nothing but their pride to make up for their sense of uselessness. That is why marriages are so unsuccessful in America, that is why your divorce rate is so high. American men don't know how to make love. You are an exception, but the average American has no experience at all. You couldn't expect to step up to an orchestra and play first fiddle without some training, but American men step into marriage without the least experience for so complicated a business. In Europe, things are different: men take the lead and that is as it should be."

"But don't you think it would be best if both partners were equal?" I asked.

"That is a practical impossibility," Freud replied. "There must be inequality, and the superiority of the man is the lesser of two evils. Though the American woman is an anticultural phenomenon," Freud repeated, "she has her good points too that one must admire: she hasn't the European woman's constant fear of seduction, for example—but she has plenty of other faults. She is discontented, too." He gave what was no doubt meant to be a typical example of an American woman who came to Vienna and ordered a fur coat and then refused to buy it, in spite of the entreaties of the poor shop-keeper.

That seemed to me to be a rather extreme type of American woman but I said nothing further on the matter.

"It is all very confusing to a young man," I said on leaving.

December 12, 1934

A sex dream—of my wife—was interpreted easily. A second dream was concerned with baggage and parcels: Ellis and I were sending a present to Freud. Since baggage and parcels were supposed to be female symbols, I ventured to say I simply wished to have some females, but Freud thought my interpretation was much too superficial. I also suggested the possibility that these parcels represented elements of my femininity, but Freud thought I was being facetious and rejected these interpretations at once.

"What put that into your head?" he asked.

"It was just a possibility I thought worth mentioning," I said.

"This is no occasion for it," said Freud.

It appeared finally that the present was a symbol for a child. "As the saying goes," Freud explained, "one *presents* one's wife with a child." The dream, then, meant that I wished a child. . . .

I went on to speak of other things and with an eye to the special interests of my fellowship, picked up the thread of yesterday's conversation. I saw no good reason, I repeated, why one ought to refrain from bisexual practices if everyone had bisexual impulses.

"Normal people have a certain homosexual component," said Freud, "and a very strong heterosexual component. The homosexual component should be sublimated as it now generally is in society; it is one of the most valuable human assets, and should be put to social uses. One cannot give one's impulses free rein. Your attitude reminds me of a child who just discovered that everybody defecates and who then demands that everybody ought to defecate in public; that cannot be. There are plenty of other impulses (*Triebe*) that we have but cannot satisfy; there is, for example, the aggressive or destructive impulse, which would be disastrous if it were not controlled. . . ."

"But that is an obviously harmful impulse," I said.

"Not at all," said Freud, missing my point, "if properly used it is absolutely invaluable and necessary to society. Our entire government, our bureaucracies, our official life, all operate on the basis of homosexual impulses, which are of course unconscious and not manifest; but there would be havoc if they were to become manifest. You cannot be a good teacher, for example, unless you have a certain amount of homosexual drive, which you sublimate into sympathetic interest for your pupils; but if the impulse were to become manifest, the effect would be exactly opposite. Bisexuality would not work, as they have perhaps already learned in Russia. Even in Greece it was discouraged."

"Perhaps," I suggested, "because of threatened race suicide."

"They did not think of such things in ancient Greece," said Freud. "To use an analogy, a man cannot keep both a wife and a mistress in luxury unless he is very rich; one of them will suffer from neglect. Heterosexuality is quite adequate for one's personal needs."

I was contented and busy reading psychoanalytic literature, I said; perhaps too much at a time, for I was sometimes perplexed. On the whole, I commented, it had a certain pessimistic influence.

"That ought not to be," said Freud.

There were so many ways of going wrong, I said, it seemed a wonder that anybody stayed normal.

"That reminds me of the Jew who visited a hospital," said Freud, "and said afterwards it was a terrible world: so many people sick (so viele Kranke) and only one healthy."

I was offended. "But it is only today that I feel halfway good," I said apologetically; "it is not always so." I went on to speak of Freud's earlier reference to my conceit, and said it may be that it was a fault in me, although I was just as often accused of excessive modesty.

"When?" asked Freud.

I told him, and spoke on, but all this was obviously superficial to a psychoanalyst and I soon broke off, not without saying, however, that such superficialities are sometimes more important for some people than their unconscious conflicts. "In any case," I said, "there must be differences in the relative importance of the Ego-development and the unconscious in different people." Freud agreed.

December 13, 1934

I dreamed that I was told that Dr. Schilder was once insane for a short period of a month or two, years ago, and recovered completely. "Did he show his latent homosexuality then?" I asked in the dream. "Yes," said my informant.

In a second later dream I was seated in the subway and saw an elderly scrawny-looking man with a thin beard sitting opposite, peering through a mask. I saw him in a double image as I watched him, then in four images, then in seven or eight images in a row, each face behind a different mask— smiling, frowning, thick and thin. I laughed in my sleep and awakened my wife. That was why I recalled the dream.

The occasion for the first dream was an article on a case of periodic schizophrenia, with complete recovery, that I had read about in a German scientific journal that afternoon.

In connection with the dream I reflected that a latent homosexuality would show itself in a psychosis. Schilder had a very high voice.

Freud made an interpretation of the first dream, which did not sound convincing to me.

"Why not simply say that it showed an anxiety that I would show homosexual traits if ever I became psychotic."

"That is your idea," said Freud. "It would be nothing new. You knew that before. I was telling you something you didn't know before because it was unconscious. You still haven't learned the meaning of 'unconscious.' "

When in the course of interpreting the second dream I said I had no illuminating associations, Freud said, "You ought simply to give your associations and not evaluate them. You seem to have no faith in the method of free association."

I gave whatever additional associations I could, and had occasion to recall all the people I had known with beards, many of whom were or had been among my heroes: such as Shaw, Ellis, Stanley Hall, and Maillol, the French sculptor.

"Who is he?" asked Freud.

I told him, but Freud had never heard of him.

"Why was it a thin beard?" asked Freud.

I did not know, except perhaps that I was once told that Ellis's beard was thinner than it used to be. Freud thereupon concluded that the dream, according to the psychoanalytic rule that all dreams in the same night pertain to the same subject, was concerned with the same theme as the first dream, but was its contrary (*Gegenstück*), as frequently happens, and was an affirmation of my prowess. The multiplication of bearded persons was the series of famous people whom I used to honor, but now mocked because they were growing scrawny and old.

Since I did not feel in the least that way about them, least of all concerning Ellis, I replied that it was at best only part of the truth.

Freud was again impatient. "The trouble is that you probably don't even believe in the unconscious: you still expect to find an agreement between a dream interpretation and your conscious thoughts."

I replied that I did believe that we had drives and impulses that did not come to consciousness, but I didn't know exactly what *the* "unconscious" was like. I expected that a psychoanalytic revelation of the unconscious would be spontaneously enlightening to the patient. How was one to know if the revelation was correct or not? This last revelation was not illuminating. How could the analyst be sure that his interpretation was correct?

"From the reaction of the patient," said Freud.

"How does the patient react when it is wrong?" I asked.

"He usually says nothing," said Freud, "because it doesn't concern him."

"But I am accustomed to respond to things that are said to me; it is only polite," I said.

"Politeness doesn't enter into analysis," said Freud.

"It is a habit with me," I insisted. "Perhaps," I added, "I have the wrong idea of the unconscious."

"To be sure," said Freud, "but what you have said has given you away."

I told Freud a little more of the interesting case report of periodic schizophrenia, with 176 psychotic attacks in twenty years, that I had been reading. The case happened to be associated with periodically increased urinary output and had other signs suggesting diabetes insipidus; later I spoke of the importance of carbohydrate metabolism in psychiatry, and gave some illustrative cases. Freud was obviously much interested, and said that was all important.

December 14, 1934

I returned the little Goethe anthology I had borrowed and said I did not think it an especially typical selection. Goethe, like the Bible, I said, could be quoted to any purpose. Freud agreed. I liked Goethe and read him with fresh interest always, I said. It was just a coincidence that I always happen to like famous men, but there was a certain sedate middle-class quality in Goethe which sometimes suggested some inadequacies. In psychoanalytic literature, too, one was often reminded of its bourgeois associations. So many of its observations came from middle-class family relations, one wondered how far they would still be true when this particular type of family disappeared. And Freud seemed to me on the whole surprisingly conservative in his morality. All this about the necessity for restraint and sublimation might very well have come from a *Kirchenbruder*, a religious moralist. In spite of his revolutionary scientific views, Freud's general outlook did not seem particularly revolutionary.

Freud agreed. "Where would we be without conventions?" he asked. "The old views and maxims had their good reasons. They weren't just grabbed out of the air. Of course, there were extremes in former days; now there are other extremes."

"Still," I said, "I am not altogether sure I understand this business of sublimation." Freud seemed willing to discuss it.

"I had once imagined," I said, "that if psychoanalysis revealed the wishes and deep impulses of people, the way would be clear for their gratification. But that doesn't seem to be the case. It still isn't clear to me why you think it is bad to be bisexual in practice, when one is bisexual by instinct. I still can't see why sublimation is so necessary."

"That depends on the amount of libido a person has available. Some have a lot, others have a little; it is a purely quantitative matter," said Freud.

"Look at Solomon," I said. "He had three hundred wives and he is reported not only to have been wise, but good. What was the use of sublimation? Married people didn't sublimate either." I didn't see that they were any the worse for it.

"That is heterosexuality that you are speaking of," said Freud. "Solomon's activities were heterosexual. I don't see where he comes in. We were discussing the sublimation of homosexuality."

"I don't understand that either. What is sublimation?" I asked. "Is it conscious or unconscious?"

"Everything is unconscious," said Freud.

"But now that psychoanalysis is supposed to have revealed my bisexual nature, does it mean that my unconscious wish becomes conscious now? That doesn't seem to happen, for I still have not the slightest wish to engage in homosexual practice. Does that mean that I have repressed the wish again?"

"No," said Freud, "the fact that a tendency has been revealed to you doesn't mean that it has to become a conscious wish. On the contrary, its force is weakened. It has less influence on you than before. You can handle it better, and are no longer at its mercy."

I went back to the other point. "From what I have observed," I said, "it seems to be precisely the people who give their impulses free play who become kindest and best-humored. It is the people who restrain themselves too much who become sour and embittered; it seems to me it is the unhappy people who are most dangerous."

"That is a valid suggestion," said Freud. "That is true, too. It all depends on the degree and quality. Everything in its proper measure. They seem to have discovered that in Russia too. At first everything was going to be free and unrestrained, but they found that it didn't work. An analyst by the name of Wilhelm Reich went to Russia and lectured there, and talked so much about promiscuity that they finally invited him to leave."

"The younger generation now seems to be rather more puritanical than we were ten years ago," I said.

"The pendulum always goes back and forth," Freud said. "Now for example the proletariat is coming into its own. It was suppressed and wronged so long; now it claims its rights and goes about suppressing and wronging the other classes. All Russia is held together by this class hatred against the other classes and against foreigners. And yet they have classes in Russia too. They have their privileged officials who enjoy all sorts of things that the workers haven't got. Go there and see for yourself. They call that progress! They don't know they have gone back thousands of years. In the old days everybody had to live together in huts, as they do now in a single room in Russia. Nobody can enjoy the luxury of a private room. What does that mean? It means the end of intellectual work. It's simply going back to barbarism."

"But that may all be temporary," I suggested.

"Of course it is temporary," said Freud misunderstanding what I meant; "next thing will be the opposite, and the other

classes will get the upper hand. But what is the good of telling that to young people: they don't see all that."

I tried to put in a good word for socialism and for youth.
"We have to have some kind of ends and ideals," I said, "or
we would never move forward. The present state of affairs is
intolerable."

"There is plenty to improve," admitted Freud. "I have
nothing against that. . . . In Italy, for example," he went on
to say, "the matches the government produces are very bad—
you can use three of them before you get a light. That is
what happens when the government goes into business.
Everything run by the government is bad. In Austria there is
a government tobacco monopoly, and the tobacco is bad. In
Holland, on the other hand, where tobacco is unrestricted and
plentiful—the Dutch don't smoke much—there is plenty of
fine tobacco. In fact, in former years, I often thought of emi-
grating to Holland. In Hamburg too, where I have often been,
the tobacco is excellent."

"Yet the government seems to do a tolerably good job with
the post office, in America anyway," I said.

"Maybe," said Freud; "but I assure you a private concern
would do no worse. People don't know what they want. Look
at Italy: for sixty or seventy years it struggled for unification.
How? It tried to unite all the Italian provinces and to elimi-
nate all the foreign ones; Austrians were driven out and were
kept beyond the borders. And then what happened? As soon
as little Italy waged its first successful war and started becoming a world power, it incorporated a purely Austrian province
in its borders, exactly the opposite of what it had done before. Ordinarily, one would say that all borders are gradual;
no matter what country occupies a border territory, there is
always a discontented minority from the neighboring country

left over, because ethnological boundaries can never correspond exactly with national territories. Italy was the one exception: the difference between Italy and Austria was knife-sharp. One could stand on a hill, as I often did, and see the Austrian houses on one side of the border and the Italian huts on the other. That didn't matter a bit, and the Tyrol now belongs to Italy. . . ."

"Don't you think there's a lot of admirable idealism behind the Russian revolution?" I asked.

"Of course," he said, "but it's an empty idealism, it's based on vacant abstractions—the same sort of thing that I criticize in your scientific views; it's not sound enough. They have a government of officials (*Beamte*) and we have a government of officials here too; that's why everything is done so poorly. A person must have some incentive to work well. They can't expect a country to survive on empty idealism. A man wants to get something for his work."

"To be sure," I said, "but it need not necessarily be money. Scientists, for example, seem to be often willing to work hard and make sacrifices for mere honor and glory. I see plenty of hard working people among underpaid doctors."

"That is different," said Freud. "People who study medicine have a thirst for knowledge (*Wissensdrang*); that is something special."

"Don't you think it possible for a factory worker to work for mere praise and self-satisfaction and distinction," I asked.

"I don't think so," said Freud. "*Ich glaube es nicht*. To close, I will tell you a little anecdote: Itzig was a little Jew who joined the army, but he didn't get on. He used to stand around and neglect his work. The powder got wet, the cannon grew rusty, and Itzig never appeared on time. He was lazy, but the officers knew that he was intelligent. One of them finally had a talk with him. 'Itzig,' he said, 'the army is no place for you. You will never get on and we all see why. I'll give you a piece of advice: go buy yourself a cannon and go into business for yourself!' " With that, the hour ended.

"*Wir werden sehen*—we shall see," I said when I went out, and Freud chuckled.

December 17, 1934

I had been reading something of Adolf Meyer's, and commented that he wrote a difficult German.

"You write admirably well," I told Freud, "and I often wonder what the origins of your style were. What were the influences?"

"Conscious or unconscious, do you mean?" asked Freud.

"I mean, what authors whom you admired influenced your style. I sometimes seem to detect Goethe's manner."

"My conscious and deliberate model was Lessing," said Freud.

"It is not an altogether typically German style either," I said. "It has none of the awkward involutions one finds so often in German writers; its lucidity is more typically French. I thought it showed some French influences too."

"Very possibly," said Freud.

I recited two dreams I had, both concerned with women acquaintances, one a friend of my wife's, another apparently a symbol for my mother. I then resumed my talk, in the old manner, of various experiences, feelings, self-reproaches I sometimes had, though nothing essentially new was brought out. "I often wonder if I am really conceited and if so why," I said.

"If you were analyzed long enough, that would all become clear to you," said Freud.

"One could, of course, simply accept oneself as one is, without understanding, and live accordingly," I suggested; "but perhaps all talk of this sort is superficial and superfluous."

"As material, it is all valuable," said Freud.

December 18, 1934

Over the weekend, I had an opportunity of visiting the Pötzl Clinik and seeing Sakel's treatment of schizophrenics with insulin, one of the most remarkable things I had ever seen. I spoke of it to Freud with great enthusiasm, and Freud was much interested. I said incidentally that it was now theoretically possible to produce a paranoia in the course of a morning with insulin and stop it in a few minutes with sugar, which seemed to disprove the psychoanalytic explanation of its etiology. Freud argued back with the greatest energy: it did nothing of the sort; psychoanalysis never claimed that there were no organic factors in paranoia, it simply indicated the psychic mechanisms behind it. A mere organic explanation would explain nothing, any more than you could explain why one drunk became manic and another remained quiet.

"All that is true," I said, "but since it is a doctor's business to cure his patients, it seems to me that the organic approach to the treatment of the major psychoses is the fruitful one."

"But analysis never undertook to cure organic cases," said Freud. I said that in New York one often saw purely organic cases that had been treated in vain for a long time by psychoanalysts, at great expense to the patients. Even epileptics are sometimes so treated.

"What your American *crooks*"—Freud used the English word—"do is certainly not representative or typical of the science of psychoanalysis," said Freud. "Analysis never claimed a prerogative over organic forms of treatment, if such a treatment is more successful; it simply assists it or clarifies it. An analyst would not undertake to cure a case of general paresis, even though he may contribute much toward its understanding. Your observations at the clinic, on the contrary, confirm the psychoanalytic point of view, for it shows that schizophrenia is functional and not fundamentally organic." Freud obviously meant organic in the anatomical morphological sense. "It is in line with the fact that schizophrenics sometimes clear up for a little while after long years of severe insanity, to relapse again soon after."

I also said one observed stages of hypoglycemia in which the patients simply seemed neurotic, and were especially responsive to psychological influence: that also seemed to suggest an organic basis for some neuroses too. Freud listened, but not altogether approvingly, I think. "It was interesting and surprising," I said, "to read in your article on psychoanalysis in the *Encyclopaedia Britannica* that you make really modest claims for the therapeutic results of analysis."

"My claims weren't so modest at that," said Freud. "I simply said analysis is not everything. There are other factors, the dynamic factors, what we call libido, which is the drive behind every neurosis; psychoanalysis cannot influence that because it has an organic background. You very properly say that it is the biochemists' task to find out what this is, and we can expect that this organic part will be uncovered in the future."

I said he only claimed success with the "milder neuroses," but Freud made it clear that he included psychoses among the severe neuroses. "Though," he added, "analysis has not been very successful with the other severe neuroses either. So long as the organic functions remain inaccessible, analysis leaves much to be desired (*lässt viel zu wünschen übrig*)."

I went on to recite a dream I had in which the Sakel insulin shock method of treatment seemed to be a failure. "This is the opposite of what I really wish," I said, "and seems to refute the theory of wish-fulfillment in dreams."

Freud argued back energetically again. "It does nothing of the sort," he said. "That is one of the apparent negatives of wishes which I have already explained and settled long ago."

"That was probably in your book on dreams, which I haven't read for years," I said.

"You probably have never read it," said Freud, but added, "If you have read it, you haven't understood it." He then gave the example of his lawyer friend's dream as it is described in his book. With the help of one or two associations, he then interpreted my dream: what I really wished was that Freud would fail in his method, and since only one of the cases in the dream was cured, that meant I was cured, or in other words successful. The dream was thus a competition dream with Freud in which I won. But when I recalled that in the dream it was *I* who failed, Freud said I simply identified myself with him.

"Perhaps," I suggested, "I wished the physical method would fail, so that I could be more devoted to psychoanalysis."

"Perhaps," said Freud. His explanation did not sound particularly convincing.

At about this time I heard from Ellis again:

Haslemere
Wivelsfield Green
December 16, 1934

DEAR JOSEPH:

I have been meaning to write before in reference to your interesting letter and enclosure. But, as usual, there is always a whirl of things to attend to.

But I am pleased to hear the Freud analysis has been going well, even though you will be glad to reach the end of it. Not surprising that it has yielded no new revelation of yourself, and you can hardly have expected that it would. But it must certainly yield a revelation of Freud and his technique, and that is what you want, and it will enable you to speak with first hand knowledge of psychoanalysis. . . .

No more now, except the best Xmas greetings to both of you from Françoise and

HAVELOCK

December 20, 1934

Today Freud was in a very good mood indeed. I commenced by saying that I dreamed I was on a skiing trip with my wife.

"Are you planning to go skiing for the holidays?" asked Freud, and wanted to know when and where we planned to go. I told of my dream, said there was a peak in the distance, where the snow gave way and slipped, and I interpreted the entire dream as showing a contrast between danger and peace: danger in the distance and peace with my wife, or, perhaps fancifully, annoyance with the analysis but inner peace and love anyway. That seemed to be the only way in which I could combine both elements. Freud accepted that interpretation, on the basis of my associations, and I went on to say that corresponded with my feelings toward him: he wasn't treating me particularly nicely, I felt, but it was perhaps my fault, and in any case, I ought not to judge him by his behavior toward me. I respected him highly as a scientist whatever his personal behavior was like, and moreover his personal behavior was probably very different with other people. I think Freud rather approved of this attitude. Freud then made it clear to me that he was not interested in criticizing me, or changing me, or passing judgment on me. He wanted to teach me and remove impediments which stood in the way of instruction.

"I do the best I can, but I always half expect you will throw me out; in fact I don't know why you keep teaching me if you find me so unteachable. Are you afraid of insulting me, or do you do it out of regard for Ellis?"

"That is one reason," said Freud, "and what is more, I don't like to give up something I have started. But you must learn to absorb things and not argue back. You must change that habit."

"I thought that to understand, is to pardon—*tout comprendre est tout pardonner*," I replied.

"This isn't a question of pardoning," he said. "It is just a question of getting on. Anyway, I am not so sure that maxim is correct. My son once undertook to criticize a German aristocrat for being rude to a lady. 'Sir,' the nobleman said, 'do you realize that I am Count von Bismarck?' 'That is an explanation,' my son said to him, 'but no excuse.' "

"What am I to do then?" I asked, "not tell you what I feel?"

"Accept things that are told you, consider them, and digest them. That is the only way to learn. It is a question of *le prendre ou le laisser*—take it or leave it. The trouble with a

Lehranalyse—a didactic analysis—is that it is difficult to give convincing demonstrations, because there are no symptoms to guide you."

"Why am I such a difficult subject?"

"I told you once before, it is your narcissism, your unwillingness to accept facts that are unpleasant."

"That doesn't sound convincing," I said, "because I have up to now heard nothing about myself which was intolerably unpleasant." So we talked on, and I finally said I would be very glad to give up my narcissistic conceit.

"That would be altogether desirable (*erfreulich*)," said Freud.

Adolf Meyer wrote:

December 6, 1934

DEAR DOCTOR WORTIS:

Many thanks for your interesting and appreciated letter that arrived yesterday.

Do not let yourself be misled by the natural concentration and limitation Professor Freud puts on himself. It is a mixture of temperament and wisdom and fate, which had best be accepted so that it gets its fullest expression. I sometimes envy that capacity; at any rate I see its great force. Actually I am able to put myself in the position of the varieties of personalities and movements without any sense of resentment, although one regrets at times the lack of reciprocity. I should give a great deal to have or to have had your opportunity so as to be in a position to be thoroughly fair toward a force that crystallized some of the most fateful meanderings—perhaps too fatefully. I understand your dilemma, but trust that you can get a most interesting sense of the principles in pure culture without loss to your ultimate digestion of it all. . . .

Sincerely yours,
ADOLF MEYER

December 21, 1934

My good spirits continued, "though I have no very good reason," I told Freud; it was quite irrational.

"It's normal," said Freud.

"Then the normal is unusual," I said. "Why?" I asked, "does psychoanalysis spend so very much time on *unpleasant* symptoms; in fact, why call only unpleasant reactions 'symptoms?' One is full of all kinds of symptoms which are pleasant." Why did Freud say it was a difficulty of the *Lehranalyse*, that one could not be guided by the patient's symptoms?

"Pleasant symptoms have not as much force (*Triebkraft*) behind them," said Freud aptly.

I recited two dreams in one of which I kissed a girl and chose her for my wife; in the other I showed my bravery in fighting a fire and in saving people. Both dreams, I suggested, were self-complacent and showed my prowess in love and life: they suggested our discussion yesterday of my "narcissism."

Freud found the interpretation satisfactory. I did not know what to talk of thereafter, and resumed our earlier discussion about psychoanalysis: it was not quite fair to refute my criticism by calling it emotional, even though I was prepared to admit an element of emotional resistance. This made things too comfortable for psychoanalysis. One might just as easily say the psychoanalyst refused to recognize just criticism for similar emotional reasons. That was no argument, but rather the preparation for an argument; one required more evidence.

Why, for example, was I willing to admit the existence of an unconscious and not the universal validity of the wish theory of dreams?

"We would no doubt learn why in time," said Freud considerately. "You must acquire more experience too," he added.

I went on to discuss my narcissism. "Why do you call it 'enviable' and at the same time try to squelch it?" I asked. "If it is enviable, then it ought to be desirable."

Freud was at pains to explain he did not mean it in any praiseworthy sense. It was just like saying of somebody, "I wish I liked myself every Sunday as much as he does himself every day."

"Moreover," I went on, "I don't see that a degree of self-satisfaction is a disadvantage; it simply means one does not waste time with self-reproach, but goes on with one's work. It seems to me, on the contrary, that one becomes kinder and more helpful to others as a result. Sometimes in the course of this analysis I have become so remorseful, self-reproachful and self-concerned that I was no good for anything." Anyway, I went on to say, I had already heard Freud criticize so many people in such severe terms, that I would hate to be included in that group.

"Who, for example?" asked Freud.

There was Stekel, for instance, I suggested. "You called him such names that I was terrified; and there was Hirschfeld, whom you called perverse and obnoxious—*einen ekelhaften Kerl.*" Freud objected to this and said he had said nothing of the kind (he had), that I did not remember what he said, and that it would be very painful to him if I repeated anything of the sort to anybody. Hirschfeld was an admitted homosexual, but Freud's relations to him were quite polite. He came to his house once, and strictly on a professional plane. Freud had simply said he was not receptive. For the rest, he was not particularly charming, as I would myself no doubt admit, and his homosexuality was not particularly appetizing (*appetitlich*).

"I am surprised," I said, "that you find homosexuality in itself repulsive."

"By no means," said Freud, "there are many homosexuals who are very fine people indeed." But as for Stekel, he went on, he knew him and worked with him for ten years, and knew what he was saying. We continued in this strain for a little while. It all reminded me, at any rate, of his critical attitude toward me.

"Your case is altogether different," said Freud, though I cannot say I found the remark consoling.

"At any rate you see," I said, "that the positive transference makes me wish you to have a good opinion of me." My good spirits were by this time gone.

December 24, 1934

On December 21, 1934 Ellis wrote, evidently in response to my account of the theoretical discussions of sex theory I had been having with Freud:

Haslemere

DEAR JOSEPH:

. . . The existence of early homosexual traits, or of an undifferentiated sexual attitude, dates from long before Freud, and the existence of very minor physical signs of the opposite sex (like the masculine nipples) makes it fairly obvious that there should be corresponding very minor psychic signs. I can trace them in myself in early life, although, from an equally early period, and all along, I am intensely heterosexual. There is no universal repression of homosexuality, conspicuously as it exists in Christendom. Nor is such repression required for a distaste to homosexuality. The homosexual component is so small, compared to the large heterosexual component, and so opposed to it, that nothing could, in the general rule, prevent the distaste arising. The circumstances in Greece were exceptional, but even there we find no distaste for marriage with a procreative object; the Greeks were thus largely bisexual. To say that the Greeks viewed homosexuality with disfavor is absurd. It is the reverse of fact! They glorified it. It was a recognized institution and the chief method of education, though not brought forward until after puberty. See the standard work on the subject, Hans Licht's *Sexual Life in Ancient Greece*. (I have never been able to find out the exact title of the German original; I have the translation.) It is a fascinating book.

Yours ever,
HAVELOCK ELLIS

When I met with Freud I told him of two simple dreams of intimacies with two girl acquaintances, and of a third dream in which I lent a certain Spanish man I knew a sum of money and did not get it back. This man had actually asked me to help him with a business letter to his bank in America, but the real occasion for the dream had been a letter from my brother asking for a loan. I had already lent him money, but had not got it back. I had lent another considerable sum to a friend in England, and to my disappointment had not got it back either, so that I was in some little money difficulties of my own. It was difficult to see how the dream was a wish-fulfillment; it seemed on the contrary to correspond perfectly with my waking thoughts and seemed a mere expression of regret; nor could I see any connection between this dream and the others, though Freud reminded me that it was a rule that dreams occurring in a single night must be related to each other. I did what associating I could, but nothing came out. If I continued associating long enough, I told Freud, no doubt something would turn up which could be appropriately used. Freud said it was inadvisable to force an interpretation, and that I had best talk on. With due apologies, I resumed the discussion of my attitude. I refused to concede that I was rejecting parts of the analysis merely for reasons of personal pride. My "narcissism" did not seem to be a general phenomenon: I stood in real awe of Ellis, for example, and trembled in his presence.

"Moreover, I do not have the impression," I said, "that you were especially modest in your youth either."

"Who, I?" asked Freud. "I had the greatest respect for the authorities of my day—until I studied things for myself, and came to my own conclusions."

"If youth did not have a certain disrespect for authority, there would be little progress in the world," I said.

"To be sure," said Freud, "but everything in measure."

I said I didn't think I felt superior to Freud; I simply preferred to be sceptical of some of his statements, awaiting proof. I did not generally stand in awe of a name simply because it was famous, but tried to judge for myself. As a matter of fact, I thought Freud was in some ways keener then Ellis, and more inclined to pursue a subject ruthlessly to a conclusion, but, I added, Ellis had a wisdom which was very profound which covered more of nature. He was a perfect type of *man*.

"To be sure," said Freud, "he is the type of the man of

culture—not really the scientific man (*der Forschertypus*)."

Ellis had written of Rank, I said; what did Freud think of him? Freud seemed at first unwilling to answer, then said, "Rank was, so to speak, my secretary for fifteen years, and was closely associated with me and did very valuable work, practicing psychoanalysis in the way it should be done. Then he went another way and since then we have no longer had relations with each other . . . I cannot go into the reasons why, because I have no right to reveal his personal life, but I can say one thing, because it is generally known: since leaving me, Rank has been having periodic fits of depression, and in between, sort of manic phases—periods in which he does a great deal of work, and others in which he cannot do any at all. He had this tendency before, but now . . . one could call him ill (*krank*)."

I neither liked the explanation, nor felt it was my personal concern, and changed the subject. "The personal factors in scientific work are certainly very great," I said, "and Meyer once wrote to me and said how anxious he was to learn what personal forces, what experiences, were behind the scientific work of Ellis and yourself."

"My personal experiences?" asked Freud. "Meyer wants to know? I certainly don't intend to tell them. No man could tell the truth about himself."

"But you could come nearest to being the exception," I suggested. "The world would be most anxious to hear, and would profit from the knowledge."

"It won't hear anything from me; I have told enough about myself in my *Traumdeutung*," said Freud. "If it discovers things in some other way, that is not my concern. People should interest themselves in psychoanalysis, and not in my person."

I said I half suspected that Ellis would write an autobiography.

"Not even he could be altogether honest," said Freud.

I said it did not seem to me to be so very difficult: whatever one revealed of oneself, one could be sure it was never completely exceptional, and it would be good if somebody undertook to break the convention of silence and hypocrisy.

"It is not a question of hypocrisy or being ashamed," Freud said. "It is simply a matter of self-protection (*Selbstschutz*), and I would not be the only one concerned."

December 27, 1934

The hour was spent in a scientific discussion of incest and the perversions. Ellis had sent me a review he had written of Westermarcks's new *Three Essays on Sex and Marriage*, and I had been thinking over this subject.

"It seems to me more likely than ever," I said to Freud, "that the sex impulse is nonspecific and changeable, not only in children but in adults too. It is kept within certain limits largely by the force of social habit and tradition, but any tradition may in time prove to be no longer useful; it is alarming to think how much the world could change if people were merely or completely 'natural'. What is really wrong with incest or homosexuality or the other perversions? What is the justification for jealousy, and supposing it comes to be recognized as wrong, what will happen to monogamy? It is disturbing to think of all the possibilities for change."

Freud said thoughtfully he was not so sure that one could call the sex impulse nonspecific, and he believed that deviations from normal heterosexuality were harmful.

"But they are harmful because they lead to conflicts with social demands," I said. "If society however did not disapprove of perversions, would they be harmful in themselves?"

"Perversions are biologically inferior," said Freud, "since they do not lead to procreation."

"But that argument can no longer be used," I said, "because the desirability of limiting procreation is now generally recognized. But perhaps I exaggerate the capacity of human beings to practice perversions; the anatomical advantages of normal heterosexual relations are so definite that they outshadow everything else."

"That may be," said Freud, "but homosexuality on the other hand is much safer; there is no danger of conception. Homosexuality, however, has other undesirable social consequences: it would disturb the ability of men to think objectively. A homosexual teacher, for example, would always show a preference for certain students, for purely emotional reasons, and it would not be the best students who would get scholarships. That is the kind of trouble we have in our university here, for example, where Christians get preference over Jews without due regard to ability."

I did not think this was a very good argument, but only said, "That sort of thing exists now in the relation between men and women, but it is not an unmixed disadvantage; in fact men and women often work together very nicely as a result."

"That is because they are man and woman," said Freud, "but a homosexual relationship would make things worse."

I persisted in my argument that it was social demands and restrictions which kept sexuality within certain channels, and quoted Ellis's statement that homosexuality was glorified in ancient Greece. Freud said it was really looked down upon by the Greeks. "One has only to read Aristophanes to see how it was regarded," he said. It flourished particularly in the old

Minoan period, but subsided later, and disappeared for unknown reasons. "But, on the whole," he said, "homosexuality seems to have been much more prevalent in ancient times than nowadays. A philosopher has recently written a book to show that all of Plato's work is nothing but an apology for his homosexuality."

Freud however was not inclined to make an excursion into sociological problems to discuss the advisability of laws against perversions, and the like. "Those are purely practical matters," he said, "and have nothing to do with science."

I did not altogether agree with this. The tenor of our discussion was not particularly pleasant. Freud sometimes did not bother to answer my remarks. At other times, he would say there was nothing new to what I said.

"Everybody knows that," he would say. I would hasten to explain I made no claims to priority; I was simply interested in getting his views.

"You ought to read what has been said on all these things," he would say. I decided Freud would have much preferred to proceed with my analysis.

December 28, 1934

Freud admitted today that the harmfulness of perverse sex behavior arose from the conflicts it caused, and that the conflicts were in turn caused by social disapproval. Since he could give no strong reason why perverse behavior was harmful in itself, it seemed to me a significant admission of the great importance of the social factor.

I resumed the account of my dreams: one dream in which I felt dirty and kept changing my shirt; another dream in which I mistook my sister for my wife, and thought of the name Oscar Wilde. By fitting them together, I said the dreams showed a wish to cleanse myself of this messy sex business and discussion of incest and perversions. Freud said fleas and insects meant children as a rule. That complicated the interpretation and we made no headway. Freud suggested that since I changed my shirt four times, the dream might be related to my four siblings—three sisters and a brother—and meant I dislike the notion of incestuous relations. I thought it might just as well mean I wished to have four children. None of this seemed convincing to me, but Freud was patient and kindly.

"When you learn more, you will be able to interpret better," he said.

December 31, 1934

"Well, what do you bring at the close of the year?" asked Freud.

I told him of some dreams. In the first, I dreamed I was driving an auto, but was making many mistakes, and almost had an accident. It was a wish-fulfillment. I wished I had an auto; I was making mistakes because it was a foreign auto, and I was driving in Austria—a nice example of a dream which seemed to be the opposite of a wish, but on close examination turned out to be one.

The second dream was more complicated: I was in a mountain hotel, among women and men resembling doctors, and a certain doctor from the eye clinic was frying eggs in the kitchen. The entire scene bore a distant resemblance to Bellevue Hospital, where I had been working, but I could not do much in the way of interpretation. I suggested the possibility of a sexual interpretation, and when I told Freud that my wife had been frying eggs lately, Freud picked up the suggestion, and said the doctor might be a substitute for my wife.

"I suggested a sexual interpretation," I told Freud, "just to show how very honest I am, and to show I have no *Widerstand*. That makes me feel there is never a completely free association; there are always elements of motivation in what occurs to me, and that ought to be taken into account."

Freud's suggestion that the egg-frying represented a domestic scene did not appeal to me.

I said in refutation that the doctor was frying too many eggs, and there were too many people around, and it was too big a kitchen for such private domesticity; furthermore, I knew the doctor too slightly and did not like him particularly. I did not know his name, but he conducted the course in ophthalmoscopy (*Spiegelkurs*). Freud then suggested that there might be a resemblance between fried eggs—*Spiegeleier*—and ophthalmoscopy—*Augenspiegeln*—which I said would be quite possible, except that I did not customarily think in German.

"That does not matter," said Freud. "All languages that you know may be used in dreams."

"Then we have been neglecting a wealth of material," I said, "for I know a number of languages."

Later Freud tentatively suggested a connection between the eggs and testicles, but I said the connection was not frequent in American parlance; the vulgar term for testicles was nuts, or balls.

"Besides," I said, "the eggs should in that case be boiled, not fried." Freud was kindly, pleasant and patient.

"Your conclusions are often more convincing than your methods," I said. "You seem to have a special kind of incommunicable intuition."

"It is not intuition," said Freud, "it is just ready association. You happen not to associate so readily where your unconscious is concerned; that is why I ventured to say you had no special talent for psychoanalysis, and that is why the process of teaching you takes longer. But some people have it, even though they may be totally uncultivated otherwise."

"Does ignorance of my own unconscious keep me from observing its workings in others?" I asked.

"That question is answered in the affirmative," said Freud. "A person who has not seen the operation of his own unconscious cannot see it in others either."

January 3, 1935

I spoke again of the insulin shock therapy, and said I found it fascinating but time-consuming; it was proving to be a serious distraction.

"I'm sure it's interesting and important," said Freud, "but you must remember you have only a month left for your analysis, and you ought to concentrate more on it. You can do the other things later. Analysis is more important for you."

"Possibly," I said.

"That is another one of your superior answers," said Freud. "You ought to make it clear to yourself that it is important for you." We argued a little about it pleasantly, and I agreed that I would spend less time on the problem of insulin shock.

"No," said Freud, "don't tell me that now. You should have told yourself that before, and never even have allowed yourself to be so distracted. Here we are moving to the end of the analysis, and you still haven't grasped the fundamentals."

I said I expected to study later and perhaps learn more when I did my own analyzing.

"But you have no right to analyze," said Freud emphatically. "You know nothing about it—you are just a *bloody beginner*." (Freud used the English phrase.) "You have no idea of technique at all. People have to be analyzed two or three years, listen to lectures, do their first analyses under control, and study thoroughly before they can call themselves analysts. You have been here a few months, and you still have to learn the wish theory of dreams and the nature of dream symbolism."

"But I cannot, unfortunately, study forever," I said. "I have a research fellowship and have to do some research of my own. What will I live on otherwise!"

"I recognize all that but it has nothing to do with analysis. You have a right to live, but not as an analyst." He then told the French anecdote of the officer who said: "*Il faut que je vive*," and the general who answered: "*Je ne vois pas la nécessité*."

"I hope that does not apply to me," I said.

"It does too," said Freud paternally. "If anybody asked me about a certain talented Wortis who came to study with me, I will say he learned nothing from me, and I will disclaim all responsibility."

"I don't seem to have made much of a personal success with you," I said.

"Decidedly not," said Freud. "I have told you the truth to the point of rudeness. It is people like you who are responsible for all the theories that are floating around, and confusing the scientific world. It is not the stupid people who cause trouble. Stupid people ruin themselves. . . . It is the people

128

with talent who cause trouble. But you are still young and can change, that is why I tell you all this."

"But," I protested, "you might have discouraged me so much that I wouldn't have done anything."

"I don't think I could have done you any harm. Either you are so conceited that my remarks don't bother you, and you run me down in return, so that I have another enemy—which doesn't matter—or else you take notice of what I say, and act accordingly. The reason for so much bad science is not that talent is rare, not at all; what is rare is character. People are not honest, they don't admit their ignorance, and that is why they write such nonsense. With young people, one has to reckon with a certain amount of antagonism, because they want to assert themselves, they want to do things better than their elders, but I, I have no reason to be antagonistic, I can afford to tell the truth, I have nothing to lose. Ellis has had a bad effect on you, because he spoiled you, because Ellis makes too few judgments, as I told you before, and here you come and feel free to air your opinions in spite of your ignorance. You say you like my conclusions but not my technique, or you say you don't believe in the wish theory of dreams." Of psychoanalysis, Freud added, I knew a *Schmarren*, which, in Austrian dialect, means a little more, or worse than nothing. "A serious scientist," he went on, "should inform himself on the subject first; you should read books on the subject—in this case, my books—and let yourself be convinced. You will find plenty of proof there from all sorts of dreams . . . a single person cannot dream everything himself. . . ."

I told of a dream I had in which I ran from one bus-line —the Freud line—to another bus-line, the Adler line, where

I caught a bus. The occasion for the dream was twofold: I had been at a party New Year's Eve at the home of Alfred Adler's daughter (who has an auto), and I also thought that Freud's emphasis of the social conflict in the homosexual problem was Adlerian.

"Do you think Adler is the only one, then, who believes that social conflict is important?" asked Freud. "Psychoanalysis has always recognized that denial of one sort or another is the cause of every neurosis. Homosexuality is not bad in itself, except possibly in a biological sense, but is bad because of the social conflicts it provokes. All this reminds me of some criticism we have been getting from communistic quarters, especially in America: they say that social factors are too much neglected by psychoanalysis. It is true that money troubles may help to complicate a situation or precipitate a neurosis, but that is not everything. But when these people start saying that the aggressive impulse comes from our capitalistic society, they are simply not scientific. If they merely said that competitive life was a factor that provoked aggressiveness, that would be something worth discussing, but matters are not quite so simple. Long ago, when I used to believe such things, I remember having two women patients in my office in succession: one a wealthy French duchess, an Austrian by birth, who bewailed her fate to me, and said at the end of her tale of woe, that she wished she had the ordinary troubles of life—a sick child, or money troubles, or a brutal husband—so that she could really feel she was a living human being, and not a mere neurotic. She went away—since I naturally could not cure her in the course of a consultation—and another woman, much poorer, came in and told me another tale of woe, about a sick husband, financial difficulties, and the like, and concluded by saying that she thought she would be perfectly all right if only she did not have these troubles. . . ."

I thought this argument had some loopholes, but did not want to pursue it. "Do you find much difference in the form and frequency of neuroses in different social classes?" I asked.

"To be sure," said Freud, "every group reacts differently."

"Are neuroses less common among the working classes?" I asked.

"Since we have opened our free psychoanalytic clinic," said Freud, "we have been able to see how widespread and frequent neuroses are among the poorer classes—but there are differences. The working man takes to drink as soon as a neurosis begins to develop, and drinks it away."

"That would seem to be a very good procedure, then," I said.

"No," said Freud, "it is very bad for the man, only it is good for the neurosis. . . . The women however have no such outlet, and neuroses are very widespread among them. In the upper and middle classes, among the bourgeoisie, on the other hand, they have their outlet in the practice of sexual perversions, which are extremely common, and in sexual excesses."

"How about the peasantry?"

"We have not much experience there, and they would seem to be less exposed to neuroses, but they have their own ways of reacting, we can be sure."

I said I would go back to New York and maybe associate myself with Schilder again if I could. "You can learn a lot from Schilder," said Freud. "Schilder shares most of our views. In some respects though, he has opinions of his own, to which every man is certainly entitled, and is thus outside the psychoanalytic group. He does not believe in the necessity of a didactic analysis, for example, and keeps his patients under treatment for only three or four months."

"Is he a pupil of yours?" I asked.

"Not directly," said Freud. "In fact, I don't think he has been analyzed by anybody, but he has lived in and absorbed the atmosphere here for years."

For some reason I had occasion to say I would consider it an honor to translate a work of Freud's. "But everything has been translated already," said Freud.

"A new work?" I asked.

"I don't expect there will be any more," said Freud.

January 4, 1935

Our New Year's greetings card carried a rough sketch of myself on the analytic couch with Freud peering over the end and his big chow sitting on his haunches beside us. Ellis wrote:

Haslemere
December 30, 1934

DEAR JOSEPH:

All best wishes for the New Year to you both from Françoise and from me. We enjoyed your clever and lifelike sketch of the psychoanalysis and laughed heartily. I hope it is now over! . . .

Yours ever,
HAVELOCK ELLIS

At Freud's I spoke again of some observations on the effect of insulin, and he followed with great interest. He agreed that it ought to prove epoch-making in medicine.

I asked whether his old observation that half of his severe

neurotic cases had a syphilitic parent still held; he said it did, though he had never worked up the material in that direction. He did not think the neuroses in his cases were due to congenital syphilis but rather to the *Keimschädigung,* or genetic taint from the parent.

I mentioned the great archaeological interest his collection of old figurines and art objects would have if it were systematically studied, as an archaeologist friend of mine had suggested, by an archaeologist with psychoanalytic training, but Freud did not warm to the idea. "These things are of interest when they are found here *in situ* and not in somebody's big private miscellaneous collection," he said.

I gave an account of a complicated dream in which I was back in America, and involved in discussions with Schilder and my sponsors concerning my plan of work. I was also in a church, and then in a courtroom in which a jolly English judge smoked a pipe. All the material came from the previous analytic hour: the discussion of my work and of Schilder. The church reminded me of Austria, which was now experiencing a Catholic revival, and the court meant I was being judged again. I suggested that the jolly judge was Freud (who also liked to smoke) and that he was jolly and tolerated a song and dance, because I wished I would be judged with levity and good humor.

Freud admitted this possible interpretation, but said it seemed too thin (*mager*) for a dream content.

I said I thought it might be sufficiently important, since it is very disagreeable to be harshly judged.

We made no further progress, and I talked of dreams in general, for I had been reading Freud's *Traumdeutung* in an earlier edition, and Freud kindly offered to get me a late edition, which he thought he had. . . . Going back to the dream, I said it was hard to say whether certain distortions in the dream were the work of the unconscious or the censor. How could one decide?

"They belong in two altogether different categories," said Freud. "One should not pair them together. It reminds me of the young lady who told the Munich hygienist Pettenkofer, 'It was all very interesting, professor, only I didn't quite understand the difference between convex and concrete.' 'The difference is the same, my dear lady,' said the professor, 'as between Pettenkofer and *Patentkoffer*'" (the German word for suitcase). Freud concluded by saying that the dream censor was not necessarily a part of the conscious mind.

January 7, 1935

I dreamed I saw a dancing troupe in Holland and interpreted the dream as a wish to see a certain half-Dutch little ballet dancer with a Dutch name I once knew. Freud agreed with the interpretation. The discussion petered out. I said I was feeling a trifle low, and Freud seemed to show a fatherly and encouraging interest.

I said the rule that all the dreams of a single night must be related seemed too rigid. "Do the people in northern Norway, where the night is six months long, have only related dreams?" I asked.

"Go up there and see!" said Freud. "Our rule is the result of our observations."

I spoke of a female transvestite that I had seen at the Bauer clinic, and Freud remarked that too little was known of female transvestitism; a case of that sort should be analyzed, he said. Hirschfeld's term was an unhappy one, he said; the cases were usually homosexual, he thought. Male transvestitism was an indication, he said, that even homosexuals preferred signs of womanliness in the men they chose—a further proof that homosexuality was seldom thorough-going. "But there are no rules," he added, "and one cannot put all cases in the same class." We again spoke of homosexuality—its undesirability, etc., and Freud said one ought not to persecute homosexuals, but one ought not on the other hand to give them entirely free rein—a certain restraining attitude, he felt, was justifiable.

A dream I had about a library and a railway station and an essay on archaeology was easily related to events and thoughts of the preceding day, but not otherwise interpreted. "The relation of dream material to recent thoughts or observations, at any rate, seems clear to me," I said.

"Even that was disputed for a long time," said Freud.

"I wonder if men who have been bottle-fed as infants would feel any interest in women's breasts," I asked.

"I think so," said Freud. "Even without assuming the inheritance of acquired characteristics, one must admit that much can be inherited."

"But I thought you did believe in the inheritance of acquired characteristics," I said.

"I do," he said, "but you don't."

January 8, 1934

This was one of the very worst hours, and I was again subjected to one of Freud's regular rough criticisms. The occasion was a dream which, I remarked rather facetiously, I was glad to say seemed quite normal. Freud made some sharp critical rejoinder, and I defended myself by saying nobody likes to hear of bad or morbid traits. Freud thereupon told me to give up my narcissistic attitude and be more receptive to what was said.

"I am not so sure I am so narcissistic," I said; "I usually don't hesitate to recite my faults and weaknesses to others."

"The reason for that of course," said Freud, "is well known: you tell other people, so that they may not tell you."

I should not argue back, he said; my incapacity to accept unpleasant facts was an especially bad trait, because, unlike other bad tendencies, it could not be diverted into useful channels.

"Perhaps I may yet find something good in it," I replied.

"Up to now I have seen no sign of it," said Freud. What was the use of telling me things like that, I asked, what was I to do about it?

"Go celebrate a Sabbath with it," said Freud, using the Yiddish phrase. I said I didn't quite know what that meant.

"Go put it in your pipe, as you Americans say, and smoke it," said Freud, in English. This was all disconcerting and got me nowhere. When I left I said I still hoped to find some good uses for my peculiarities.

"It is certainly to be hoped for," said Freud.

I had also reported another dream, in which it seemed to me I killed two people. "An annoying dream," I remarked.

"Annoying to the people, you mean," said Freud.

January 9, 1935

Freud was very nice today and spoke in a friendly interested tone as soon as the analysis started. I warned him that I was very much tempted to fight back after yesterday's humiliation, though I realized that my knowledge of psychoanalysis would not be thus improved. Freud however encouraged me to let off steam, and said he would not take offense. I said in brief I thought his methods of arguing were intimidating and coercive, and that he did not allow me enough freedom of discussion or opinion, etc., etc. Freud answered with admirable patience, said he did not wish me to accept his views at once, would rather have me be sceptical and cautious, only he did not want me to reject them at once, either; that he did not mean any personal offense, that he did not wish to overemphasize any particular abnormal tendency of mine, that I was well within normal limits, and that everybody showed one tendency or another.

I told him of a dream in which I was back at Bellevue talking in a friendly way to Schilder; it seemed to reflect the spirit of my own wishes regarding Freud.

January 10, 1935

I had another dream in which I was talking amicably with Freud, and admiring his vigor. Freud was again friendly and attentive, accepted my interpretation of the dream as a wish for conciliation but added later it seemed at times *too* friendly and suggested an overcompensated hostility. He took occasion to put in a little word of praise for me here and there, and offered me a copy of the recent edition of his *Traumdeutung* that I had been looking for.

He recently had occasion to ventilate again his homosexual theory of jealousy or lack of jealousy, and had cited Dostoievski as an example of a man who gave his wife freedom of conduct with a beloved male friend. Last night I had two dreams in which I made love to the wives of friends. I said it looked as if I accepted his theory that a man may grant his wife freedom with a beloved friend, provided that it was I who played the part of the friend.

"That is much more satisfactory," said Freud, and accepted my interpretation.

The conversation turned again to insulin and psychiatry. Freud again stated his position on organic factors in neuroses and psychoses, talking clearly and deliberately. Analysis, he said, was limited in its curative effect because it could not reach the organic factors, but it recognized the importance of such factors. A constitutional organic factor was not necessarily something unchangeable. He welcomed the advent of insulin shock treatment, and thought it meant progress, but said there was nothing revolutionary to the idea that schizophrenia could be cured, since spontaneous remissions were known to occur. "A disease that can cure itself can be cured by medicine too, that is a general rule; medicine is an aid to the natural forces." Not all such aids were equal in value, he went on to say; there were degrees of potency. He told me of a case of melancholia in a woman where the symptoms disappeared completely for an interval of three weeks, because the woman's child contracted diphtheria. He mentioned cases of hysterical paralysis where the paralysis disappeared in an emergency. "Not all psychic influences," he said, "are equally potent. As Charcot always used to say, 'We cannot compete with Lourdes'; and many cases indeed were actually sent there. In analysis however we have the powerful tool of the unconscious."

I said on leaving that it would be good if all psychoanalysts showed his open-mindedness and good sense in these matters.

"If they are my pupils, they do," said Freud.

January 15, 1935

I had a slight cold and did not feel in a mood to discuss the intricacies of my personal life. I told of a simple dream the night before, in which I got involved with three women, including my wife.

"An easy dream," said Freud, "showing infidelity and fidelity at once."

"A typical dream of mine," I said, "which I have had very often." I talked of odds and ends, not much to the point, and Freud made little comment. I remarked that artists for some reason seemed to me sometimes to be more intelligent than scientists, but Freud said nothing. I spoke of my liking for music, which was not easy to understand in terms of the unconscious. Freud suggested it was a satisfaction of some deep craving for rhythm, but admitted that the problem of esthetics in music was very obscure. Bauer, I told him, counted the love of music among the degenerative stigmata.

"An exaggeration," said Freud. I also said that Bauer always insisted that a lingua plicata generally was an indication of neuropathy. Freud did not know what a lingua plicata was. I explained. Freud was interested but unimpressed, and agreed with me that it simply meant the tongue was a bit larger than the jaw containing it. About Bauer, he said a person may have talent in one direction and be a fool in another. Before leaving I asked whether he thought all this chatter was a sign of resistance.

"I think so," he said. "Tomorrow we may pretty surely expect it to become so clear that we can attack it."

At about this time I wrote a letter to Dr. Meyer which reflected my feelings toward some of my current experiences:

Dear Dr. Meyer:

There has been much of interest that has turned up lately, and now that we are leaving soon, I have less time than ever to catch up with myself. Freud continues to teach me patiently and on the whole sympathetically, though every two weeks or so I get a humiliating scolding for being too sceptical. Freud has a wonderful talent for making one feel worthless, and if I took everything he said seriously, without analyzing *him*, I should feel pretty low indeed. It will soon be over, and it will have been a fine experience.

Last time I mentioned Stekel's name to Freud, Freud cursed him roundly and took three days to forget it, but today I met Stekel in the *Gesellschaft der Ärzte* and took a little walk with him. Stekel seems to be an interesting man (he spoke enthusiastically of you), but all these schools of analysis are simply confusing to a mere beginner, and the amount and intensity of personal animosity I find among them has no parallel except perhaps among opera singers. It seems to me that the reason for this is that psychology is far from being an exact science (I am doubtful if it can ever be) and leaves much room for personal preference and prejudice. I think, though, that the scientific part of psychology can be much extended, and already there seems to be a conflict between some clearly demonstrable facts and psychoanalytic theory.

I should like to call your attention, Dr. Meyer, to a remarkable contribution to the study of schizophrenia, which is now appearing in installments in the *Wiener medizinische Wochenschrift*. It is concerned with the effect of insulin hypoglycemic shock on early schizophrenic cases, and is by a young Austrian internist named Manfred Sakel. The first installment appeared, if I remember, in November, 1934 (No. 45), and the series is still running. I have been checking up on his claims and following up cases of his at the Pötzl Clinic for the past month, and find everything he says reliable: the results are simply *extraordinary*. Pötzl is now behind him, and if the procedure is developed it may well prove historical. I am doing a report in English to bring back with me. The procedure at present is very difficult and dangerous and there have been two deaths this past year. It is beginning to be widely discussed and ought certainly to prove important. Freud is much interested.

I manage to get to Bauer's a few times a week and am busy with the little *Arbeit* that Marburg suggested to me. His valuable little seminar is continuing and information pours in from all sides at once—perhaps more than is good for me.

Tomorrow my wife and I shall lunch at Marburg's. He was very pleased to get your regards again. We are planning to leave about February 1st, or as soon afterwards as we can, and it ought not to be long before we see New York again. What my plans will be like then it is difficult to say, but in a general way my work is now laid out for me, and I have plenty to think about. I ought to be seeing —— early in March, and hope you will find time to see me when I get back.

Sincerely,
JOSEPH WORTIS

January 16, 1935

After meeting Stekel at the Medical Society I had a dream about him. In the dream he proposed a new theory for the origin of homosexuality, saying it came from an otitis media, and travelled over the nerve, like a filterable virus, to produce brain disturbances, resulting in homosexuality. Freud said an organic point of view was foreign to Stekel's nature; whatever he was it could be said to his credit that he remained an analyst and his outlook was analytical. In the dream I rejected the theory, and said I would wait until I found a convincing one. This, I said, corresponded to my waking thoughts about psychological schools in general.

I said Stekel described Freud to me as "one of the greatest of geniuses," but Freud rejected the compliment by saying it was purposely meant to reach his ears. "Calling me a genius is the latest way people have of starting their criticism of me; that is the sort of thing that has been happening for the past five years or so. First they call me a genius and then they proceed to reject all my views. If they thought I was a genius, one should think they would not question my authority. If they said I am a genius *because* I discovered dream interpretation, or the meaning of symbols, or the phenomenon of repression, then I would be satisfied. But they do just the opposite."

"But," I objected, "you certainly consider many people geniuses but still reject their views. I am sure, for example, you think Goethe a genius, but you do not accept everything he said."

"To be sure Goethe was a genius," said Freud, "but he was a poet, not a scientist."

"Or, take Charcot," I went on. "When you were not much older than I you wrote a fine appreciative essay on Charcot, in which you rejected some of his views. Charcot still thought, you remember, that general paresis was an inherited disease."

"It's true I criticized Charcot," said Freud, "but not on my own authority. I simply took sides with Fournier against him on that point. But," he went on, "it's true I took an independent position against him on some points too, on his emphasis of heredity and so on. . . . But with you," he continued, "it is not a question of taking sides or forming independent opinions; you reject views simply because they are unpleasant. That is not a scientific attitude."

"I am sorry if I have ever pretended that it was; and if I did, I hope I have changed," I said. "But it would be worthwhile," I added, "to review the things I have rejected simply because they were unpleasant."

"There haven't been too many," said Freud, and made some reference to an earlier dream interpretation. I concurred in a spirit of sincere conciliation.

"But in analysis," Freud warned me, "one learns what real conviction means, and I think there is reason to suspect that you are still not altogether convinced."

"Because," I interrupted, "I was too proud to present you with an apparently contradictory dream?"

"Fine!" said Freud with enthusiasm. "That's what I call real analysis."

"Well," I said, "I hope I will learn in time."

"That was fine!" said Freud again.

January 17, 1935

I was reading a volume of Einstein's in the waiting room when Freud came in.

"Einstein is an interesting and likeable man," I said, "but his attitude towards the Jewish question is somewhat puzzling to me, and I confess I am not easily in sympathy with his or your Jewish nationalism. I wish I could clear up the problem for myself. I have no strong Jewish feelings, and up to recently was satisfied to think of myself mainly as an American. How far ought I to let my allegiance to the Jews bring me?"

"That is not a problem for Jews," said Freud, "because the Gentiles make it unnecessary to decide; as long as Jews are not admitted into Gentile circles, they have no choice but to band together."

"But how about the program for the future? I would like to see the Jews become assimilated and disappear, and Einstein talks as if they ought to be preserved forever."

"The future will show how far that is possible," said Freud. "I personally do not see anything wrong in mixed marriages, if both parties are suited to each other, though I must say that the chances for success seem greater in a Jewish marriage: family life is closer and warmer, and devotion is much more common. My married children have all married Jews, though it may be that they would have married Christians if they had found the right ones. It simply happens that the Gentiles who courted them or with whom they came in contact were not up to standard, and the Jews of their circle seemed superior. It may well be however that they simply did not have access to the best Christian circles. There is no reason why Jews ought not to be perfectly friendly with Gentiles; there is no real clash of interests. But a Jew ought not to get himself baptized and attempt to turn Christian because it is essentially dishonest, and the Christian religion is every bit as bad as the Jewish. Jew and Christian ought to meet on the common ground of irreligion and humanity. Jews who are ashamed of their Jewishness have simply reacted to the mass suggestion of their society."

"But I don't know what the Jews stand for," I said. "I can pledge allegiance to a scientific group, or a political or cultural group because they represent certain ideals, but what does Judaism stand for; in what way do its ideals differ from other group ideals?"

"Ruthless egotism is much more common among Gentiles than among Jews," said Freud, "and Jewish family life and intellectual life are on a higher plane."

"You seem to think the Jews are a superior people, then," I said.

"I think nowadays they are," said Freud. "When one thinks that ten or twelve percent of the Nobel Prize winners are Jews and when one thinks of their other great achievements in sciences and in the arts, one has every reason to think them superior."

"Jews have bad manners," I said, "especially in New York."

"That is true," said Freud; "they are not always adapted to social life. Before they enjoyed emancipation in 1818 they were not a social problem, they kept to themselves—with a low standard of life it is true—but they did not go out in mixed society. Since then they have had much to learn. In countries where they have enjoyed real freedom, however, as in Italy, they are indistinguishable in this respect from Italians. The old saying is true: 'Every country has the Jews that it deserves.' America certainly hasn't encouraged the best kind of social conduct."

"It is also said that Jews are physically inferior," I said.

"That is no longer true either," said Freud, "now that the Jews have access to outdoor life and the sports, you find them the equal of the Gentiles in every respect, and we have plenty of champions in all fields."

"And, finally," I said, "the Jews are over-intellectualized; it was Jung who said, for example, that psychoanalysis bears the mark of this Jewish over-intellectualization."

"So much the better for psychoanalysis then!" said Freud. "Certainly the Jews have a strong tendency to rationalize— that is a very good thing. What Jung contributed to psychoanalysis was mysticisim, which we can well dispense with. . . . But I do not want to go too much in the direction of nationalism either," Freud continued. "I am not much of a Zionist—at least not the way Einstein is, even though I am one of the curators of the Hebrew University in Palestine. I recognized the great emotional force, though, of a Jewish center in the world, and thought it would be a rallying point for Jewish ideals. If it had been in the Uganda, it would not have been anything near so good. The sentimental value of Palestine was very great. Jews pictured their old compatriots wailing and praying as in the olden days at the old wall— which by the way was built by Herod, not by Solomon—and felt a revival of their old spirit. I was afraid for a while though that Zionism would become the occasion for a revival of the old religion, but I have been assured by people who have been there that all the young Jews are irreligious, which is a good thing. . . . But all this," said Freud, "is not psychoanalysis; however it is worth discussing because I see you have a sincere interest in the problem. Besides it has its psychoanalytic value too: people are after all nothing but children, they believe their parents more than anybody else. If one takes a parental attitude, it is all to the good. People tend to believe those people whom they love or like. It ought not to be so, but it is."

I told of a dream in which I met Magnus Hirschfeld (whom I once met casually) in a bookshop, and discussed

sex problems with him. I suggested that the dream was analo-
gous to yesterday's dream about Stekel; both were critical of
Freudian psychoanalysis, and both people were disliked by
Freud.

"But Stekel is not homosexual," said Freud, "by no means.
He was quite a seducer (*verführerisch*) in his youth, which
I do not hold against him—it was perfectly all right. Hirschfeld is not only homosexual, but perverse too, and in the
most ludicrous way. . . ." Freud then proceeded to tell me
in detail of the way in which Hirschfeld satisfied himself
with male prostitutes, with an elaborate ritual involving pressure on his toes, etc. "What could be more ludicrous and
childish?" concluded Freud, and he then explained it all psychoanalytically.

"I must confess that I find it difficult to judge," I said.
"All I can say is that it seems strange, but I think evaluations
are out of place. How do we know what high thoughts they
have during this procedure?"

"None, I can assure you," said Freud; "even in normal
coitus, one shouldn't have high thoughts, one's only interest
is the act itself . . . It's true that evaluations (*Werturteile*)
have nothing to do with science, but science need not prevent
us from making them. Anyway, it is childish and unde-
veloped." Freud then gave some other ludicrous and obscure
examples of perversions. "If you think all those are biologically or esthetically equal to normal coitus," he concluded,
"that is your privilege."

"It's all a matter of private taste," I insisted. "Bernard
Shaw calls meat-eating disgusting cannibalism, and would
probably find it hard to understand how a person can chew
a dirty cigar for hours on end."

"That is true," said Freud, "but you could say that meat-eating and smoking are at least universal habits, but those other things are not."

January 18, 1935

I dreamed last night appropriately enough of a slaughter-house and its brutalities. Beyond saying that it was worth serious discussion, neither of us had further comment to make, and I went on to other themes. I talked of various melancholy thoughts about the world and my future and the meaning of life, but agreed that these preoccupations were not of great importance, and probably came from the slight cold and malaise I was troubled with.

"Those are problems that everybody has," said Freud, "and are not personal problems of your own. . . ."

For lack of subject matter, I revived yesterday's discussion and said I could not agree with Freud's attitude towards the perversions; I felt they were a purely private concern.

"To be sure they are," said Freud, "but that does not mean that they are beyond criticism. Homosexuality is another matter, and stands on a higher plane, since it is capable of different uses, but even that ought not to be accepted as equal to normal." I said homosexual interests were so often found in men of the highest type—Leonardo, Whitman, Edward Carpenter—that it was difficult to look upon them as something inferior.

"But an inferior trait doesn't by any means exclude the presence of the highest kind of qualities," said Freud. "If you go out to the Rothschild Garden here some day in the Hohe Warte you will find certain fruit trees of stunted growth which yield the most glorious and perfect fruit: it is often through some such sort of compensatory system that such achievements are possible. People of high intellectual ability are very often sexually abnormal or inadequate. Impotence is common, or the sexual impulse may be very weak altogether. Homosexuality is common too. Leonardo, for example, was probably an *ideal* homosexualist: that is, he probably was homosexual by nature but did not actually exercise his homosexuality. Socrates and his circle were certainly homosexual, and probably Plato too. . . . The presence of some such trait certainly does not exclude the highest type of ability . . . Kant," Freud went on, "seems to have been quite asexual, and the German artist Menzel actually declared in his will that he had never had relations with either man or woman."

Freud was very glad to hear my wife was pregnant. "It is high time," he said.

January 18, 1935

Some simple dreams about girls were quickly disposed of. I also returned to an unexplained dream of the night before, in which I made some purchases of books and ropes— reminiscent of our old backyard, where I used to climb; and where foreign currency and figures occurred—reminding me that I was leaving soon for Germany and home. I suggested that the dream showed a wish for more physical action such as climbing, and an interest in going to Germany and seeing R. Freud was satisfied.

I talked a little of my plan of work in America, said I wasn't particularly keen on the subject of sex psychology or homosexuality and hoped I would find other fields to work in too. Freud said homosexuality could be an extremely interesting subject. I discussed a case history of a homosexual that I had just received from Ellis: the subject was narcissistic, longed for his childhood again, and felt an attraction to boys of eleven who resembled himself as he then was. He had been circumcised for medical reasons at the age of eleven and was only interested in uncircumcised boys. Freud explained the case very aptly, said it was a transparent case of fixation at a certain age, that the homosexuality was here closely associated with the narcissism, and the subject really wanted his *former* self back again. Analysis was indicated: perhaps the fixation could be made fluid again and the subject would grow interested in older mates and have a chance to achieve some satisfaction. Relations with children ought not to be encouraged or tolerated, said Freud; in fact they ought to be prevented with the severest measures. Nobody ought to be permitted to have sexual relations with people who did not enjoy freedom of choice and judgment: an employer, for example, had no right to make advances to an employee, because free choice was not possible there. Children were still in the formative period of their sex development and ought not to be exposed to perverse influences; at the age of sixteen or seventeen, however, the sexual direction had been pretty much established, and relations were much less harmful. . . . I asked Freud how the high frequency of homosexual practices among the aged—especially toward children—could be explained. Freud said, "With the declining intelligence of the aged, there is also a diminution of moral restraint, and old latent tendencies which have all along been lurking in the unconscious now break through and show themselves. There are other factors too: perverse practices were less dangerous, and moreover old people have less opportunity for normal gratification . . . In fact, there is a general moral deterioration in old age," said Freud. "The old saying that youth has no virtue (*In der Jugend gibt's keine Tugend*) is just the opposite of the truth: *only* in youth does one find virtue. The older you get, the worse (*boshafter*) you become. Women are especially awful in old age. It is said that women are the best examples of love and human kindliness, but that applies at best only to young women. When a woman begins to age, she becomes an awful example of malevolence and intolerance. In fact I do not think that men are in this respect much better: they are intolerant, ill-tempered, petty-minded and unkind to an extraordinary degree."

"But not all of them," I said.

"What?" said Freud.

"Not all of them," I repeated.

January 21, 1935

"An acquaintance of mine," I said, "a rich American woman, is now in her fifth year of analysis."

"She must be rich to afford it," said Freud.

"The question is, how far do analysts yield to the temptation to keep their patients overlong."

"It is a question of medical ethics," said Freud. "Abuses are possible in analysis as in other branches of medicine."

"Except," I said, "for the special weapon of the positive transference. At any rate, it raises the whole question of the importance of money to patients in analysis."

"Now that we have free clinics and the psychoanalytic institutes, the question no longer arises. Anybody can now be analyzed; they may have to wait a little, but everybody has the privilege. Besides, every analyst has a number of free patients. Here in Vienna, for example, every analyst undertakes to treat two free patients. When one considers that an active analyst can at best treat seven or eight patients at a time, then you must appreciate that it means a considerable sacrifice."

I spoke of the place of psychoanalysis in socialized medicine, but Freud did not like the notion.

"It is not suited to state supervision and has found no place in the social insurance schemes here; the present system seems best, and there is no occasion to worry about it. Psychoanalysis is not a field where one grows rich easily."

Freud spoke of the special nature of psychoanalytic practice. "One soon learns to be attentive to hours of narrative without a strain," he said. "It is only original thought which is tiring. When you simply play a passive part, it is no different from sitting in a railway carriage and watching the landscape roll by; one soon learns what is significant and worth remembering, and it is always interesting."

I asked Freud whether he found writing difficult.

"No," he answered, "because I have usually not written until a thing was ripe and I felt a real compulsion to express myself. When I have had to write to order on the other hand —introductions and the like—it has always been hard."

The only dream I could remember was concerned with a medical school for women, and with libraries, both suggesting an interest in certain women doctors I knew, especially in F.

January 22, 1935

Two scanty dreams concerned with the insulin cure and with hunting were inadequately interpreted, and I went on to talk of hunting.

"The dreams are often simply an introduction to the other material," Freud reminded me.

A professional friend happened to be discussing his favorite sport of hunting with me the day before.

"I like hunting, except for the shooting part," I said.

Freud said the love for hunting was a residue of the old hunting instinct from which men once lived; in modern times it seemed superfluous and sometimes simply barbarous. "Sadism is all right in its place," he concluded, "but it should be directed to proper ends."

I ran out of conversational material, but Freud again reminded me I was to talk of simply anything—science included—that occurred to me. "Otherwise," he said, "the analysis would be of no value at all." I spoke a little while of the new insulin treatment, and he said that showed at least where my interests lay. I then went on to speak of my analysis in retrospect.

"We are approaching the end, and it may be worth-while to look back in review," I said. I had heard more bad things about myself than good, and my spirits were perhaps dampened, but on the whole it looked as if I would leave the analysis as healthy as when I took it up.

"But you still have time for the funeral oration (*Leichenrede*)" said Freud. "We have another seven hours or so, and plenty can happen by then; all this simply shows that you are anxious to get it over with."

"Or else," I suggested, "I want to give you a chance to put in a few good words for me before it is over."

"That is not my business," said Freud. "I told you unpleasant things about yourself to show you how honest one is in analysis."

"It is said of the people of Yorkshire," I said, "that they always tell the truth, provided it is unpleasant."

"Exactly," said Freud, "if it were merely pleasant you would suspect that it was just flattery."

"But if it is all too unpleasant, one suspects the motives too," I said. "I sometimes get the impression that I must somehow be worse than other people."

"Then you don't know what other people can be like," said Freud. "I have told you one thing and another about yourself, but I do not wish to exaggerate its importance. It is true you have no palpable symptoms, but you have no right to be too proud of your health. Everybody has some slight neurotic nuance or other, and as a matter of fact, a certain degree of neurosis is of inestimable value as a drive, especially to a psychologist; and it is on the other hand possible to have strong character defects inside the limits of so-called health. . . . I feel sure, for example, that Ellis must have some sexual abnormality, else he would never have devoted himself to the field of sex research. You might of course say the same of me, but I would answer that that is first of all nobody's business, and second of all it is not true. I was drawn to study sex by my study of neuroses—it was years before the importance of sex dawned on me. In fact on three separate occasions I had been told of the importance of sex in the neuroses, without ever reacting to the suggestion." Freud for the next twenty minutes told me in detail of his experiences with Charcot, Breuer, and others, exactly as he has told them in his *Zur Geschichte der Psychoanalytischen Bewegung*, repeating Charcot's "*—la chose génitale—toujours—toujours—toujours*" with great dramatic emphasis, and reciting the exact Latin description at the end. But I was too annoyed with what he said about Ellis to be very attentive. He was not only wrong, so far as I knew, but he was being vulgar and unfair.

"I hope," I said when I left, "that people won't speak of me as you speak of Ellis."

Freud was by this time however deeply immersed in his own past, and simply shrugged his shoulders.

January 23, 1935

I had four dreams last night and told Freud about them. In the first, I made love to a girl friend of my brother's.

"Was your brother present," asked Freud.

"Fortunately, no," I said. Freud laughed.

In the second dream, I attempted to interest Stephen Spender (whom I had met some time before in Salzburg), Mrs. ———— and a certain woman doctor in myself by talking about Freud. "He is in very fine condition," I said in the dream, but what I meant to say was, "He has a very fine intelligence." The woman doctor in the dream said I used an awkward phrase, but I stuck to it and tried to justify myself. I said to Freud that I considered this an example of paraphasia in dreams, of the kind Kraepelin wrote about. Freud said Kraepelin's paper was trash (*einen Stiefel geredet*) and it was just an ordinary slip of the kind he described in his *Psychopathologie des Alltags*; the organic factor was simply negligible; there must be other factors involved. Freud at this point had again begun to tap on the head of the sofa, as he always did when he was impatient and displeased.

In a third dream, I came upon a scrapbook full of literary essays by an ambitious acquaintance, Dr. B., written under an assumed name. This was an identification with myself for I hoped to write literary essays some time too, perhaps under a pseudonym.

In the fourth dream, I was slipping into my high school classroom late and with feelings of guilt, and hid myself in a corner seat out of the teacher's gaze. All I could say about this dream was that it suggested the discomfort I felt when Freud spoke as he did about Ellis.

"It was just a supposition," said Freud. "It is not the sort of thing I would write an essay on."

I said that was the sort of lay opinion that made Ellis's life so difficult and cheapened his accomplishment. Freud then gave the reasons: I had said his wife was homosexual; besides, he had no children, and a man who makes so few judgments is suspect of being impotent. I insisted I never said his wife was homosexual; so far as I knew she wasn't.* He had no children because his wife was diabetic—besides, he was too poor; and as for the last argument, it was weak. Shakespeare made few judgments too—he saw too many sides to an argument.

Freud was angrier than I had ever seen him. He sputtered: "Do you know Shakespeare, then, as well as you know Ellis? Anyway, he was a poet, not a scientist." Besides, what did I mean by now denying that his wife was homosexual?

I could not say what I meant for I did not remember—I could only suggest that a certain woman friend of his, who was heterosexual, once had a brief experimental homosexual period. If Freud had read the Ishill book in his waiting room, he could himself have seen from Ellis's little prose poem, "A Revelation," that he was not impotent. Freud had me go into his waiting room for proof, which I produced, but which did not satisfy him, for there was no clear evidence of a sexual

* Freud must have acquired this information from another source, for with the later publication of Ellis's *Autobiography*, there appeared to be some justification for this characterization of Edith Ellis.

156

act. "I would advise you to be more cautious (*gewissenhaft*) hereafter in your statements."

"One can never be too cautious," I said.

January 24, 1935

Freud was remarkably friendly today and chatted pleasantly as soon as I began to tell my dreams: they were concerned with traveling at high speed to a kind of barracks where Nazis were billeted, and the whole dream seemed rather tense and anxious. I suggested it all came from thoughts about the quarrel yesterday and thereupon, of course, the discussion was renewed. Freud emphasized that he did not mean to deprecate Ellis in the least: Ellis was a wonderful man, etc., and he had the highest regard for him: he had simply ventured a certain supposition based, as he now saw, on incorrect evidence, and he took it back. There was then some discussion back and forth about the actual statement, and the evidence, and so on. It seemed that I was especially prone to say inaccurate things in the course of an argument; it was a bad trait and I should exercise more caution. I said I considered myself punished, and Freud said mildly I deserved it.

"Everybody is liable to have some personal reason for choosing a particular field of work," he said; "it is not a rule, but it is frequent." His daughter's ophthalmologist, for example, had trouble with his eyes, that was why he became an eye doctor.

"It is also said," I replied, "that psychiatrists are half-crazy, ought one to believe that too?"

"There is a lot of truth to it," said Freud, "though Wagner-Jauregg is an exception—he is perfectly normal." Freud then told me of how his friend Wagner-Jauregg was forced against his will into psychiatry from his chosen field of pathological anatomy. "The result was," said Freud, "that he limited his interest to the organic part of psychiatry, where he made very important contributions. . . ."

"And would you say that most psychoanalysts are neurotic too?" I asked.

"Many of them are, in fact a great many; only one can say that neuroses are so very widespread nowadays that the difference is not very great. Besides, a certain amount of neurotic stuff gives a person the necessary interest and drive in his work."

I didn't like the idea of these group diagnoses, and said it makes it hard for a person to feel that he is in a marked group; it multiplies his conflicts: the Jews for example are more liable to neuroses because they are looked upon as inferior.

"I am not so sure of that," said Freud. "Gentiles have plenty of neuroses too. Only the Jew is more sensitive, more critical of himself, more dependent on the judgment of others. He has less self-confidence than the Gentiles, and is fresher—has more 'chootzpa' too—both come from the same thing. Jews are less sadistic than Gentiles, and the neuroses in general develop themselves at the cost of sadism: the more reckless a person is, the less neurotic. Besides, the Gentiles drown their neuroses in alcohol, and the Jew does not drink."

Anyway, it was all disturbing and confusing, I concluded, and one wished that one could work without being bothered and distracted by personalities.

"I am sick of fighting," I said, "and I don't know why we have so much of it."

"For cultural reasons," said Freud, but I am not sure I understood.

"If I were left alone," I said, "I would be the most harm-
less of animals."

"And do you think you are the only one?" asked Freud.

January 25, 1935

Dreamed of making love to F., while her husband sat in the
adjoining room with my own wife; this little touch, I suggested, preserved the equilibrium of my married life, and
satisfied my sense of justice. My brother sat watching disap-
provingly through the front door, and represented my own
conscience. In a second dream, my wife and I passed B. and
H. on the street, each of these with a girl, though H.'s girl was
B.'s wife, Miriam. These latter two made love to each other,
which embarrassed us, though B. attempted to take it lightly.
The best I could do, by way of interpretation, was to suggest that my own contented married life was a pleasant contrast to all this.

Freud accepted the general interpretation, but said it was
all too simple. "A dream ought not to be too simple," he said;
"every dream ought to disclose a secret."

I had recently seen a demonstration of hypnosis, and Freud
told me how hypnosis was the phenomenon which first convinced him of the existence of the unconscious and stimulated the first growth of psychoanalysis. He told me in vivid
detail of the demonstration of Bernheim at Nancy, especially
of the phenomenon of post-hypnotic suggestion. Bernheim
had told a man, for example, that he would open an umbrella
and walk around the room with it on awakening—which the
man did, and then attempted to explain rationally: he just
wanted to see if the umbrella was intact. When Bernheim insisted however that that was not the real reason, the man
slowly and with difficulty finally said he was doing it upon

command; this proved to Freud that it was possible to elicit unconscious material by coaxing and encouraging a patient.

"There has to this day," he said, "never been a better demonstration of the existence of the unconscious than the phenomenon of hypnosis. When philosophers talk about the impossibility of the unconscious, one can only advise them to witness an hypnosis; but people don't want to be shown— that is the way human beings are."

We talked for a while of various hypnotic physiological phenomena: catatonia, the production of blisters, anesthesia, pallor, etc. But Freud was not friendly to an emphasis on organic factors. "It is superfluous and gets us nowhere," he said. Of hysteria, he said, "It is the one neurosis where the organic background is relatively insignificant."

We talked of hysterical fits, and I said the transition to real epilepsy is only gradual, and sometimes the two were alternate in an individual, or indistinguishable. Freud thought that merely showed the psychic factors in epilepsy were underestimated. "It used to be said," he said, "that Dostoievski was an epileptic, but we now know that he was a genuine neurotic and merely had hysterical seizures."

January 28, 1935

I dreamed a simple sex dream, involving a little girl friend of C.'s. "Since you suggested the triangle situation to me," I said, "I have been making active use of it." In another dream, on the following night, I found myself in Moscow, which seemed very pleasant. I suggested that it was simply a utopian dream, but Freud thought the interpretation was too thin. "There must be something more to it," he said. My talk waned, and I started repeating myself, wandered off into discussions of one thing and another, and ended with a profession of my love for music. I had just bought tickets to *Don Juan* and said it was one of my very favorite operas.

"That is no wonder," said Freud. "It is the greatest opera there is."

January 29, 1935

The conversation was lagging. I dreamed of walking with a friend of my brother's while he flirted with some girls—a reminiscence from New York. Beyond saying it was a pleasurable reminiscence, I could not revive much more pertinent material.

I commenced again to talk of one thing and another, and ended up again in politics. A Communistic psychoanalyst had recently written that Freud had overlooked the importance of the class basis of society. "He exaggerates more than a little," said Freud. Freud praised Marx for elucidating the materialistic side of history—"but people go too far with it," he added.

"The same as with psychoanalysis," I said. "As soon as a great discovery is made, it becomes popular and exaggerated, and there is more than a superficial resemblance between Marx and Lenin and their disciples, and Freud and the other so-called psychoanalysts."

Freud made no comment. I spoke of Trotsky, who had spent a number of years in Vienna.

Freud said he knew he spent much time in the Café Central, in Adler's circle, but he had never met him. "Communism and psychoanalysis go ill together," he said.

I spoke of Walter Lippmann, who, Freud said, had once called on him. "He has a beautiful wife," said Freud.

"What's your impression of him?" I asked.

"That's not my field," said Freud. "He's an economist."

"But he has written books on morals and the like too," I said.

"I don't take them seriously," he said.

I talked some more of politics and wealth, and told him how they kowtowed to me at the big bank down the street when I wanted to cash a big check.

"It's natural for banks to like people with money," said Freud. "The trouble is, it happens outside of banks, too."

And finally, as I was leaving, he said: "I don't think that Communism is the hope of the future. (*Ich glaube nicht dass der Communismus das Heil der Zukunft ist.*)"

January 30, 1935

I dreamed of calling on Dr. B. in his research laboratory back in New York and of seeing his cousin Dr. N. who was active as a surgeon. The dream suggested an interest in both kinds of work, and anticipated my return to America. During the rest of the hour I reviewed point for point the things I heard about myself in the analysis, starting with Freud's depreciatory remarks about my abilities. Freud listened without much comment, except that he softened the effect here and there, and made the criticism seem purely objective. I then went over to his description of my character traits, and he again made little comment. I proceeded to the more intimate knowledge of myself and to some of my psychological tendencies. Freud said this was merely a description of my character type and ought not to be overestimated; it was a narcissistic deficiency which he could not explain. I went on to say that though he detected one or another distasteful element in my dreams, they seemed to me to be quite strong in their normal content. "Too strong in fact," said Freud. I therefore considered myself a fairly typical person in these respects. "That is quite possible," said Freud. "But this kind of discussion," he added, "does not fit into analysis really. Analysis tries to avoid every kind of suggestive influence and does not undertake to make judgments or give advice."

January 31, 1935

I had met Stekel again briefly and again told Freud how highly Stekel spoke of him. "It is all a pose," said Freud. "He plays the respectful disciple and meantime assumes the privileges of a superior. He forgives me, so to speak, for all that he has done to me." Freud then told me of the old fights, not only between himself and Stekel, but between Stekel and Freud's other pupils. One of these pupils (who since committed suicide) set about to prove that Stekel was a liar, and according to Freud succeeded.

"It is disconcerting to see so much animosity among scientists, and I do not look forward to having similar experiences," I said.

"It is unavoidable," said Freud, "and one had best prepare oneself for it."

"One would think," I said, "that differences of opinion should not prevent a friendly relation."

"One ought to expect it, but it is unfortunately not so," said Freud. "But it is not the scientific differences that are so important; it is usually some other kind of animosity, jealousy or revenge, that gives the impulse to enmity. The scientific differences come later."

Since this was my last hour, I dreamed, appropriately enough, of saying good-bye to Freud in a friendly informal way. A grandson of his in the dream declared his intention of studying medicine, then analysis, but I told him, "The name of Freud is sufficient. You don't have to do anything more."

In the dream I felt like a bad schoolboy, and I suggested that the guilt feelings came from the sense that I did not do well in the analysis.

"What makes you think that?" asked Freud.

"It is just my feeling," I said. I summarized my feelings: in spite of things I had to hear about myself, I was glad that I had made the acquaintance of a great man—"But," I added, "perhaps I ought not to use flattery."

"Go on," said Freud. "One is free not only to go to the one extreme, but to the other too."

I said there was enough truth in what had been said about me to give food for thought. Of analysis, I had learned enough to understand its methods and techniques, and to value its scientific earnestness.

"That is the main thing," said Freud. "I am glad," he went on, "that you have taken everything in this friendly spirit."

In my dream, I asked Freud for a certain favor . . . perhaps a photo. "If you mean that seriously," said Freud, "I can only say—though you may not believe me—that I don't possess any. But I have books and I would be glad to give you one before you leave." He then gave me a copy of his *New Series of Psychoanalytic Lectures* and wrote his name in, at my request.

"I will just write the name," he said; "I do not usually like ceremonials."

I said too that his views on socialism had been important to me and we spoke of that for a while.

"I find capitalism quite satisfactory," said Freud. "I think the discovery of money was a great cultural advance; to return to trade by barter is simply a slip backwards. To be sure, one ought to regulate the production and distribution of wealth more satisfactorily, but it is difficult for me to see in advance how that can be done. Perhaps we may have to await scientific advances before any real improvement is possible. The cost of Communism to intellectual freedom is too great. Communism means an intellectual dictatorship; it is not compatible with psychoanalysis because it is too dogmatic. Reich, a talented psychoanalyst, will probably have to leave the movement, because he has turned Communist and altered his views. He believes, for example, that the aggressive instinct and sex problems are products of the class struggle, instead of products of inborn biological drives." Freud then spoke of the necessity of having a private room and the right to be alone occasionally. "That in itself is enough to make Communism impossible for me."

I said that my father could never enjoy such privacy because he had to work fourteen hours a day all his life in his shop.

"That need not be so bad," said Freud. "It depends how he takes it. There are rich people who travel around all the time who are profoundly unhappy. I have not left my room, for example, for months. For years I used to take a walk every day from two to three o'clock after my coffee, but now I am willing to stay here, contented in my little prison." But Freud acknowledged the force and importance of Communism. "It will take centuries, though," he said, "before its value can be extracted and enjoyed. Communism, like Christianity, always promises the people a better world in the future, to repay them for their misery. The only difference is that Christianity promises it in another world." We chatted for a while longer, Freud sent his warmest regards and best wishes to Ellis through me, and wished me a good journey.

BACK HOME

SOON AFTERWARDS my wife and I moved homeward through Berlin. The burly porter at the *Bahnhof* told us that things were getting better in Germany, now that the Jews were being ousted. We met friends and new acquaintances in hushed circles exchanging stories of new harassments and depredations under the National Socialist regime; several were preparing to leave the country. We visited a blond physician who headed a tuberculosis sanitarium on the outskirts of Berlin, dined with his fair-haired wife and four blond children, talking of trivialities until he accompanied us at dusk through the flat countryside to the station, greeting the passers-by with "Heil Hitler!," confiding to us just before we left that he was deeply committed to the anti-Hitler opposition; but even his wife did not know. In London we again met Ellis and Madame Cyon, and then went home, to new work at Bellevue, where I resumed my relationship to Dr. Schilder.

Though Ellis was just recovering from a winter siege of illness, he remained alert and busy, and we maintained our correspondence. A visit to the opera where I saw Wagner's crooked dwarfs protecting the Rheingold suggested an analogy, which Ellis then commented on:

Haslemere
Wivelsfield Green
Hayward Heath
March 9, 1935

DEAR JOSEPH:

. . . It is satisfactory you do not regret your stay in Vienna, and the contact with Freud was invaluable whatever your opinion of him. When you speak of "the strenuous and crooked creatures bearing the precious Rheingold" I think you are symbolically describing what genius so often is. I have often referred to this aspect of genius (perhaps suggested to me by Hinton)—its foundation in deformity, one-sidedness, unbalance, the ability to see the new thing accompanied by the inability to see the old. You see *I* am not troubled by genius. When Olive Schreiner first knew me (I was 25) she thought I had genius; a few years later (without any change in regard for me) she came to the conclusion that I hadn't. Your Rheingold symbol is admirable. I don't mean that it would necessarily apply to all men of genius. There is, for instance, Einstein, one of the greatest, who seems quite harmoniously developed. Do you know Michaelis's book on "Freud"? Rather interesting and suggestive. He admits Freud's greatness, compares him indeed with Nietzsche, but emphasizes the "crookedness" and one-sidedness of his outlook, and regards him as a disappointed idealist who has taken to systematically repressing his idealism.

. . . I wonder if you have seen Rank—and detected his manic-depressive tendency!

Affectionate regards in which Françoise joins.

HAVELOCK

Soon after my return I had sent the complete batch of closely written index cards comprising my analytic diary to Meyer for his perusal. He read them eagerly and wrote:

The Johns Hopkins Hospital
Baltimore, Maryland
May 1, 1935

DEAR DOCTOR WORTIS:

. . . Your notes with Freud are one of the most naturally convincing and illuminating documents or memoranda that I could conceive of. It all rings very true to my own thought of Freud. Evidently, there was a great deal of surrender of dogmatism and a great deal of mutual frankness that forms a real contrast to a good many of the reports that one occasionally gets. I think you had a most interesting opportunity and you have used it well. Like so many other things of the kind, one regrets that there was not more of it and that some of the very vital claims could not have been discussed to the end. Somehow, I feel that the relationship between you gives a fair amount of justification for assuming that a good many highly dogmatic assumptions and conceptions would have been similarly liberally treated. . . .

Most sincerely yours,
ADOLF MEYER

At about this time I sent a brief farewell note to the aged Freud, to which he responded.

Vienna, IX, Berggasse 19
July 14, 1935

DEAR DOCTOR WORTIS:

It is true that your analysis with me was *no immediate success* [note that Freud used the English phrase]. But your

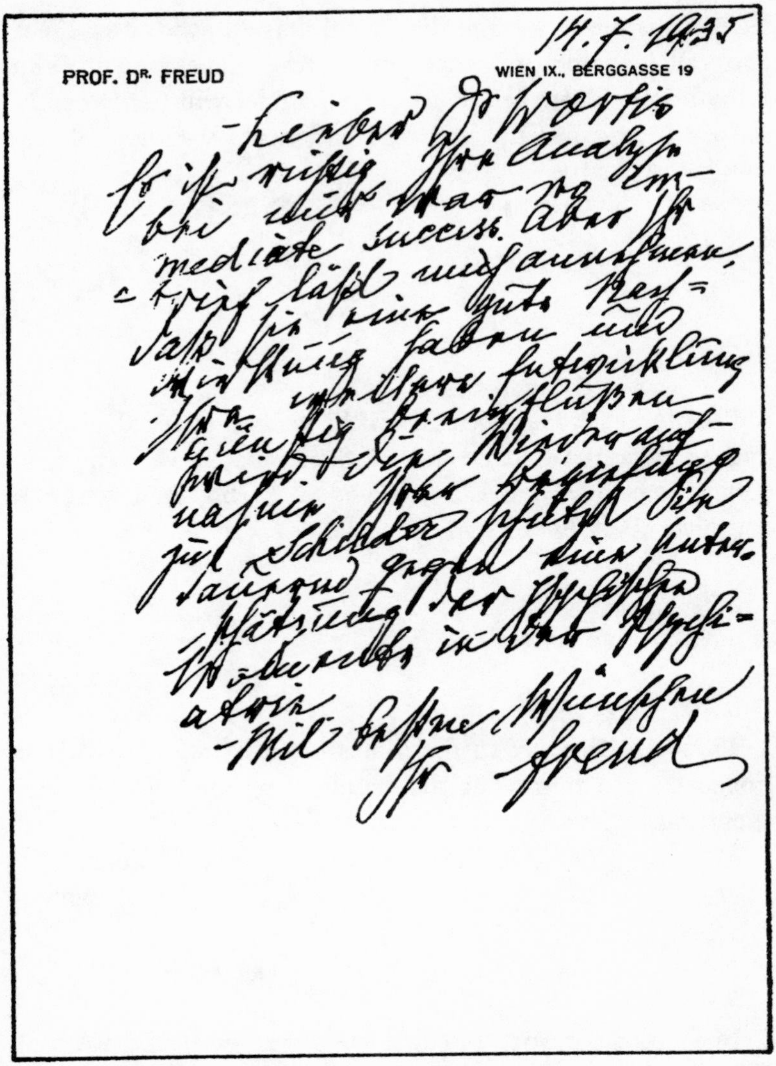

14. 7. 1935

PROF. Dr. FREUD

WIEN IX., BERGGASSE 19

Lieber Dr Wortis

Mit besten Wünschen

Ihr Freud

letter leads me to assume that it will have a good after-effect and will favorably influence your further development. The resumption of your relationship to Schilder will permanently protect you against the underestimation of psychological factors in psychiatry.

With best wishes,
Yours,
FREUD

I wrote to ask Havelock Ellis if he wanted to see the notes, and he answered that he did. In September, with some misgiving, since I valued Ellis's judgment so highly, I sent the complete diary on to him.

September 10, 1935

DEAR HAVELOCK:

These are the day to day notes—as they were written. I hope you can make out the handwriting, and do not find them too tedious.

Yours,
JOSEPH

In October of 1935 our first child was born and we sent Freud an announcement. He answered graciously: "my greetings to the young citizen of the world!"

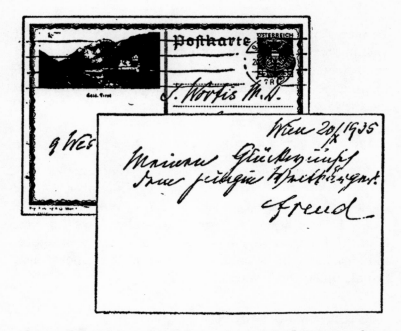

Meanwhile I began to work at a few scientific papers of my own, and got deeply involved in the excitement of introducing shock treatment in the U.S.A. Ellis was reading my Freud notes at a leisurely pace, and late in October wrote:

> 24 Holmdene Ave. S.E. 24
> *October 29, 1935*

DEAR JOSEPH:

   . . . I have been reading more of your Freud notes and finding them extremely interesting, full of instruction and suggestion. And I am always much more in sympathy with your attitude than with Freud's. The notes seem to me a severe criticism of the technique. Like you, I cannot attach great importance to "repression" in a normal person and what may superficially seem so in a child is merely a secondary result of the normal impulse of imitation. And I agree with you that what one says, if told to talk at random, is influenced, indeed completely controlled, by one's consciousness (and unconsciousness) of the person who is listening. Replace the listener and the talk would be completely replaced. . . ."

And a few weeks later he wrote:

Haslemere
December 2, 1935

DEAR JOSEPH:

. . . I am still reading your Freud notes. They are most valuable, I suppose a unique record of Freud's technique, and must certainly be published, sooner or later, though not, I think, under your name. . . .

Soon afterwards he wrote:

Haslemere
February 1, 1936

DEAR JOSEPH:

. . . I continue to read your Freudian notes (as does Françoise) with much interest, and wherever you differ from Freud I am nearly always on your side.

There is one point, where I am concerned, at which Freud seems to have gotten into a muddle. He said that I wrote a letter of protest to him about a criticism of me written by Jones. But I am quite indifferent to criticism, and never in my life sent such a "protest" to anyone or even dreamed of doing so. I recall the real facts. Jones in his journal wrote a long review of my Vol. VII [of "Studies in the Psychology of Sex"]. I glanced at it, saw it was in his most superior and supercilious tone and never read it through; have not done so to this day. But Françoise read it, and seeing that Jones had treated me as actively hostile to Freud, she thought that this might offend Freud, and *on her own*, wrote a note to F. to the effect that Jones had quite misrepresented my attitude to him (Freud). This was the supposed "protest" by me! It would of course have, anyhow, been absurd to send a protest to one man against a criticism written by another.

But this letter is already too long. . . .

Françoise joins in affectionate greetings to you all.

HAVELOCK

And finally, amidst many troubles and distractions, Ellis wrote:

Haslemere
Wivelsfield Green
Haywards Heath, Sussex
September 14, 1936

DEAR JOSEPH:

I have finished reading the Freud notes with much interest, and, since the packet is rather awkward for mailing, Mrs. P——, who leaves England this week, has kindly consented to take the packet to you and I have today sent it to her in an envelope fastened up and addressed to you.

I consider the notes most valuable and that they ought, *some day*, to be published, after Freud's death, and perhaps anonymously. They do not, however, reveal anything about you. Their value is that they constitute *an analysis of Freud,* and a precise revelation of his technique. I do not suppose that any similar record—even if it exists—will be published, as the ordinary patient would not of course care to give himself away, not even anonymously.

I am almost afraid that the notes might in a future age be regarded as a *reductio ad absurdum* of psychoanalysis: But, *anyhow*, they will be valuable.

Various points crop up in the notes that I want to write to you about. But they must wait awhile. I am busy trying to

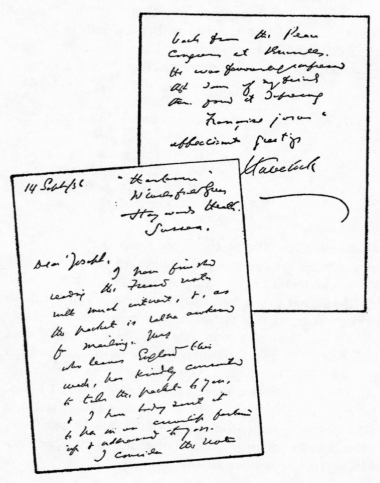

settle up things, as we go to Cornwall early next week. . . .
Françoise joins in affectionate greetings,

HAVELOCK

Two weeks later Ellis wrote from Cornwall:

October 2, 1936

DEAR JOSEPH:

We are spending a fortnight in Cornwall by the sea, near
the Lizard, an old haunt of mine, and enjoying, strange to
say, quite splendid weather, and we take what I call long
walks (ten miles or so) and I am feeling very well, being
always better for the sea. Françoise also is at her best.

You will doubtless have safely received the Freud notes
from Mrs. P. I think they constitute a valuable document, to
be carefully preserved for some future use, as an illustration
of Freud's technique. I noted a number of interesting points,
and there seem to be contradictory statements. At one point
F. says that dreaming thought is a continuation of waking
thought; on another occasion that it is "essentially different."
To me it has always seemed that the dream processes—the
feelings and the logic—are the same, but under new conditions—and that makes all the difference. I accept the per-
petually shifting scene, however absurd, presented to my
dream consciousness, but I react to it with the same likes
and dislikes, and the same logic, as in waking consciousness.
The difference is great, but I doubt if it can be correctly
termed *essential*. It is a difference simply due to dissociations
which doubtless have a physiological foundation. Of course I
would say that F. drives symbolism to death by assuming its
existence everywhere. Symbols may enter into sleeping consciousness, as into waking consciousness, being based on re-

semblances, and of course they were recognized long before F. (Ferrero's almost earliest book, forty years ago, was on symbolism and I almost put it into my Science Series; Ferrero came to see me about it.) But to say, for instance, as you represent F. saying, that falling in dreams is symbolic is not only improbable but merely freakish. My most pronounced experience of this is very ancient, but it lasted all night, so that I have never forgotten it. I was assistant to a doctor at the time, who gave me a large dose of chlorodyne on account of an attack of haematuria which I had contracted through standing in his cold surgery. All night long I was falling, falling, falling. No doubt F. could furnish a brilliant symbolic interpretation. But the real reason was the sensory anaesthetic effect of the drug mixture. In the slighter casual falling dreams that sometimes occur it is natural to suppose that there has been some sensory pressure of the body in a cramped position acting similarly. The "falling" is of course still a symbolism, but a rational symbolism, the absence of any realized contact, and the sense of space, produced by the anaesthesia, being symbolized by the falling. I wonder whether the extraordinary exuberance of psychoanalysts in fantastic ideas is not largely a manifestation of repression: a repressed artistic impulse here finding an escape which it regards as legitimate. F. was rather indignant (perhaps a suspicious circumstance!) when I once told him he was an artist. But he is an artist!—I sometimes feel I would like to sweep away all the existing psychiatries, and begin again on a strictly biological foundation. I am not sure that a good grounding in botany might not be the best approach to psychiatry. And the more or less complete absence of consciousness in plants should make it easier to resist some of the temptations that afflict the psychiatrist. A lot is now being learned about plants. And they act exactly as we should in their place, with the endless individual differences.—Your notes, you see, are most suggestive!

I am interested in F.'s remarks about me, and not at all annoyed at the suggestion that my interest in sex was due to a perversion. It is precisely my own feeling about many sex-obsessed people, and it is often correct. But I am quite ready to accept F.'s statement that it was not true of himself. Neither is it true of me! I was only sixteen when I resolved to make sex research a main object in my life. And I meant *normal*, not abnormal, sex. At that time my own experiences of sex were *entirely* confined to the distant worship of one or two girls and to emissions in sleep, which I found a worrying phenomenon. All the books I could see (I might say all the books that existed) on sex were superficial, prejudiced, fantastic, or goody-goody. Krafft-Ebing's book was first published just about that time, but I did not know of it till later and, anyhow, it would not have helped me, being nearly all pathological. I knew nothing whatever about abnormal sex and was not interested in it.—As regards my wife, she was not diabetic until the last years of her life, but was neurotic, and her constitution in various ways fragile, and before marriage the wise old physician in whom she had much faith had advised her against having a child, and we adhered to this view, though at one time we were inclined to re-consider it. (My own spermatozoa looked quite healthy under the microscope!) As regards the "Revelation" in *Impressions and Comments*, F. is quite right; there is no coitus, real or assumed, in the narrative. The "Person" in question, I may now privately mention (though when she last came to see me she said, not long ago, that she no longer minded being recognized in it) is H.D. I had, in the first place, obtained her consent to print it, with some difficulty, though she said, when I read it to her, that it was so beautiful it almost brought tears to her eyes, and it is generally considered by critics my finest piece of poetic prose. H.D. has told me that at that period I was an immense help to her—I have never known why—and she remains an affectionate correspondent. With regard to impotence, F.'s notion that it is associated with a lack of decision in intellectual judgments is new to me. The notion seems based on a false analogy. In most of the cases that come to me, the impotence is not due to any hesitation or lack of decision, but is a hyperaesthetic over-rapidity of nervous reaction, reaching its climax before entrance is effected. I am accustomed to associate it with the excessive rapidity of nervous reaction marking the whole of our modern civilization; I don't imagine the stolid peasant easily becoming impotent. (Freud has himself somewhere ingeniously argued that with the growth of civilization the sexual instinct, both in men and women, will tend to be repressed and perhaps lead to the extinction of the race.)

And if we do assume that impotence is more than an involuntary nervous phenomenon, then what we would expect on the voluntary intellectual plane would be an Adlerian "masculine protest"!—an over-emphasis of decision. Indeed it may be plausibly argued that this is just what we do find. There is some reason to suppose that Carlyle and Ruskin were impotent, and both of them are conspicuous in their emphasis of intellectual affirmation.

I fear that to me your psychoanalysis of Freud seems rather damning! Indeed I am a little inclined to agree with McDougall about "the greatest figure in psychology since Aristotle"—who is nearly always wrong! But I do *not* agree with McDougall that he himself anticipated Freud. That is absurd. Freud is an extravagant genius, McDougall is merely pedestrian.

This is for me a long letter. But it is your notes which are responsible!

Affectionately ever,
HAVELOCK ELLIS

I kept thinking about the content and meaning of my psychoanalytic experience and thought for a while of resuming my personal analysis and joining the psychoanalytic movement. I discussed the matter with Dr. Meyer, who encouraged me to continue. I wrote to the late Dr. A. A. Brill, Freud's translator and an early psychoanalytic pioneer, who answered (December 5, 1936):

. . . . I certainly would agree with Dr. Meyer on your didactic analysis. In your place, I would make arrangements to continue it here. I will be very glad to cooperate with you on that matter.

Cordially yours,
A. A. BRILL

But the exciting and promising demands of other work and interests, the scientific independence that my fellowship allowed, and a growing scepticism toward psychoanalytic doctrine all led me from that line of development, and I found plentiful opportunities for useful work elsewhere.

In March 1938 the Nazi armies marched into Vienna. Soon afterwards, according to the *New York Times*, Freud's home was visited by the Nazi secret police and then by storm troopers. His passport was lifted. Freud's safety and life seemed threatened by this new barbarism and some of us tried to bring some pressure of public opinion to bear upon the situation. At Bellevue Psychiatric Hospital a statement was prepared and signed by nearly every member of the staff, from the director down, and forwarded to the President of the American Psychiatric Association, to our State Department and to the German Embassy:

> We members of the staff of Bellevue Psychiatric Hospital of New York City earnestly request the American Psychiatric Association to record in the name of American psychiatry its vehement protest at the brutal treatment of the aged scholar Professor Sigmund Freud by the Nazi invaders of Vienna.

Among the thirty-five signers of the statement were: Drs. Karl M. Bowman, Paul Schilder, Lauretta Bender, Frederic Wertham, Walter Bromberg, David Wechsler and Frank Curran. The President of the American Psychiatric Association thereupon issued this statement for transmission, through our State Department, to the German Foreign Office:

> Speaking in the name of American psychiatry for 2,000 American psychiatrists, I voice our earnest hope that everything possible be done to protect Professor Sigmund Freud of Vienna from disturbance. Professor Freud, who has contributed so magnificently to medicine and to the welfare of humanity, is a sick old man: His hundreds of friends in America are deeply concerned about him, beg that every consideration be given him and that his home be kept peaceful.
>
> Ross McFie Campbell

In May, Freud, after a payment of a huge ransom by Marie Bonaparte, was allowed to leave Vienna for his beloved England. Ellis, meanwhile, in failing health, had moved out of London to Suffolk; Ellis and Freud exchanged a few more letters but never met. I made a short visit to England in 1938 to see Ellis once again, was also tempted to visit Freud, but felt hesitant about bothering him. Ellis wrote to me in London:

> Cherry Ground
> Hertleshorn, No. Ipswich
> *August 6, 1938*

. . . . I have not been able to see Freud, though he has asked me to come. He is unable to go out but seems pleased to see visitors. His address is, as you may know, 39 Elsworthy Road, N.W. 3. I don't think you would bother him.

> Yours ever,
> HAVELOCK

I decided, however, against seeing him, and returned home soon after.

Ellis died in July, 1939. Two months later Freud died, worn out by prolonged illness, but spared the additional painful experience of living through another and more terrible world war. Meyer retired in 1940, and soon afterwards was disabled by his fatal illness. Schilder, Stekel, Rank, Adler, Brill—all passed on. A new generation of psychiatrists moved forward, with no one to lean upon any longer but themselves.

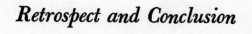

Retrospect and Conclusion

How would I characterize my relationship to Freud? Freud was a person of resolute honesty, motivated not only by an intense scientific curiosity, but by a high level of human feeling as well. He had learned to be a fearless fighter, and fought hard even when there was nothing to fear. A young man coming to him from so far and under such grand auspices, who cockily rejected him, must have been peculiarly provocative. Old age and many infirmities had already depleted his energies and probably contributed to his irritability. Nevertheless I think that if I could have accepted his scientific creed I would have enjoyed his friendship, and would have gravitated toward a professional career of considerable convenience and comfort.

Though I approached the analytic experience with scepticism, my attitude towards it was frankly curious and I was willing to be shown. The series of inept and inappropriate interpretations early in the analysis (that a house represents the womb, that a stage show represents coitus, etc.) and the general foraging in a false direction indicated to me as the analysis went on that I was not likely to get any deep or valid insights from it. Actually I think a dividing of the ways came at about the middle period of the analysis when I began to realize that people by and large must work their problems out in the arena of real life and action and not by endless probing into the reaches of an obscure unconscious repository of instincts and childhood repressions. There is no doubt that Ellis strongly reinforced my resistance. The trouble basically however was that I could not accept Freud's scientific views because both his approach and his conclusions were suspect to me. This is not to say that in many matters, great and small, he was not right (as he certainly was in many of his comments to me), but the psychoanalytic structure as a whole seemed rickety, infirm and without solid foundation. To those who may be quick to conclude that it was the personal difficulties which led to these scientific differences, I would simply say that basically it was the scientific differences that caused the difficulties.

This intimate account of conversations with a great man, of comments heard in the unguarded moment, no doubt has its interest and appeal to those who want to know what Freud was really like. The record easily revives my own vivid recollection of the old man, but much of it still bores and bothers me: the bickerings and repetitions, the sensitivities and apprehensions and the rude exchanges now offend my sense of propriety, and make me wish we had behaved better. Yet under the circumstances I do not know how I could have done differently; the picture of an uncertain, sceptical, stubborn, but candid and serious youth stands as it was, true to the facts. I resist the temptation to be drawn into a defense of that record: let others do so if they wish. It must be conceded that the level of disputation maintained during the analysis cannot meet scientific standards nor settle the issues involved. It seems worth while, however, to note some of these weighty scientific issues that stare you in the face on nearly every page:

There is the bold assertion of Freud's that the scientific objections to psychoanalysis rise from the subjective fears and failings, largely unconscious, of the critics.

There is the constant concern and preoccupation with unconscious material, and relative neglect of consciousness, of the vicissitudes of daily life, of experience.

There is the explicit belief in the importance of biological instinct endowment, of the universality of innate bisexual drives, of aggressive impulses, and even of an inherited propensity for hunting, for the use of certain dream symbols, etc.

There is the conviction that social feeling and social integration derive from sublimated sexuality, rather than from mutual interdependence and economic need.

There is the acceptance of male dominance, and of female subjection, on biological grounds.

There is the historical pessimism and low estimate of man, also on biological grounds.

There is the great concern with dreams, as the true indicators of the unconscious, and of the true nature of the subject.

There is the belief in the wish theory of dreams, in the universality of certain dream symbols, and in the validity of free association in interpreting symbols.

There is the preoccupation with the transference.

There is the belief in mental telepathy.

There is the conventional morality.

Overriding everything else, there is the basic psychoanalytic conviction that the personal subjective and internal factors are more important for the understanding of both the individual and his society than the objective and impersonal: it is man with his poor and blind endowment of unconscious biological drives who makes history and not the social processes of history or of experience which make man.

Any single one of these propositions is worth an essay or a treatise, and the whole subject of psychoanalysis deserves much fuller treatment than this book allows. The issues cannot be decided by an easy appeal to the experts, because the experts disagree. Readers who wish to inform themselves more fully on the scientific differences involved will have to read Horney, Fromm, Pavlov, Schneirla, Sears, Bartlett, Sherif, Cantril, and many others. In the years since Freud's death the fortunes of the psychoanalytic movement have prospered and waned in different parts of the world (and lapsed in certain countries completely); yet psychoanalysis is now enjoying a greater influence and prestige in contemporary America than it has ever had elsewhere before. A wider participation of thoughtful people in the discussions will promote more clarity in this area and help resolve the disagreements.

My own attitude toward psychoanalysis took more definite shape as my experience enlarged in the ensuing years. When, after my return to this country, I thought of resuming my analytic training, I well knew that my contacts with Freud would be regarded in my profession as an auspicious start. I was also tempted to think that the differences in point of view that were emerging among American psychoanalysts would favor a more liberal attitude toward individual opinion than Freud was able to evince. But the cleavages in the American movement soon took sharper form. Schilder was forced to leave the Psychoanalytic Society in New York, and was followed afterwards by Karen Horney and her pupils. At least half a dozen more or less distinctive psychoanalytic groupings began to take organizational form on the local scene. For a period I felt that Karen Horney was supplying a refreshing new social emphasis, but later I came to think that she too maintained the essential errors of the psychoanalytic tradition, without the attraction of Freud's original and fascinating subtlety of formulation and invention. In 1945 I contributed a critical essay on "Freudianism and the Psychoanalytic Tradition" to the American Journal of Psychiatry, which represented, in brief, my attitude toward the subject at that time. I might now modify some of those conclusions in detail, but still believe the critique is basically correct. To round out the record, it seems proper to conclude with some such brief credo of my current views:

Psychoanalysis certainly reflected a fresh and useful point of view when it first emerged as a scientific movement half a century ago. At a time when psychiatry was bogged down as a science and had become much too interested in merely labeling and classifying psychological disorders, psychoanalysis boldly sponsored a new individual and biographical approach to the understanding of psychological problems. It opposed the harmful habit of looking upon these disorders as something fatally or mysteriously fixed and static, and depicted individuals in their process of growth and of change, molded by their endowments and past experiences, and spurred on by their peculiar drives. Freud presented a kind of dialectical picture of personality, as composed of many conflicting tendencies, both good and bad, and scorned the simpler formulas of common parlance, or of the fashionable science of his time.

Psychoanalysis thus helped develop a new science of mental function—psychology—at a time when psychiatry was dominated by the mechanical materialism of the pathological anatomists, or the experimental laboratory interests of the early psychologists. It strengthened scientific materialism at a time when religious idealism was influencing certain schools of psychiatry. In those early days it encouraged a spirit of therapeutic optimism instead of the fatalism or nihilism then prevailing. It helped shatter the taboos against an examination of sexuality and the family. It made a penetrating and subtle analysis of many psychological mechanisms that had been previously neglected or unknown: repression, projection, sublimation, regression, transference, reaction formation, etc. It presented a realistic picture of many sordid aspects of the contemporary personality and family. It accumulated a vast wealth of observational data on human personality.

Freudianism however did not escape the influence of its own social and historical origins and had certain basic defects from the very beginning, which at first impeded its development and later led the psychoanalytic movement into theoretical formulations and attitudes which cannot be regarded as valid or useful.

The only honest and proper way to criticize a scientist is to take his data or his conclusions piece by piece and prove them true or false. Since we cannot do that now, I can only summarize what I think have already been proven to be the basic failings of Freud's theories. In essence they reduce themselves to his failure adequately to recognize man as a social animal, whose qualities and drives are quite unlike those found in non-social organisms. Freud's persistent interest in reducing human thought and behavior to innate instinctive drives, or to early childhood fixations or repressions, or to the operation of an unconscious that makes no contact with reality—all of this, and much besides, has led Freudianism into more and more abstruse and mystical formulations that have not only confused both social and psychological issues, but have even prevented psychoanalysis itself from making a suitable self-examination of its own social origins and significance. But if we look over a few psychoanalytic beliefs or formulations, their social implications (and social origins) can easily be detected. For example:

1. *Psychoanalysis believes in the preponderant influence of the unconscious.* Freud believed that the behavior of people, in general, is not motivated by a correct and realistic appraisal of an actual situation, but essentially by innate instinctive drives, modified by early experience (in the first years of life) and only slightly influenced by later experiences. So far as any particular situation is concerned the behavior of people must be regarded as irrelevant

and irrational. According to one prominent psychoanalyst, Erich Fromm, for example, the German people when threatened with fascism identified their fascist leaders with their fathers and yielded to them: ". . . Many of the adherents of the leftist parties, although they believed in their party programs as long as the parties had authority, were ready to resign when the hour of crisis arrived. A close analysis of the character structure of German workers can show one reason—certainly not the only one—for this phenomenon. A great number of them were of a personality type that has many of the traits of what we have described as the authoritarian character. They had a deepseated respect and longing for established authority." (*Escape from Freedom*, pp. 80-81.)

For adults the Freudians believe in the ascendency of outworn unconscious ideas over actual situations. For children they believe in the ascendency of instinctive drives over actual situations. In both cases the Freudians assume an ascendency of ideas over the realities of a situation. Many people nowadays have come to see that it is not primarily the ideas of men that determine their way of life but, on the contrary, the mode of their existence that determines their ideas. Freudianism believes in exactly the opposite relationship. In a typical passage Freud declares: "It is quite impossible to understand how psychological factors can be overlooked where the reactions of living human beings are involved; for not only were such factors already concerned in the establishment of these economic conditions, but, even in obeying these conditions, men can do no more than set their original instinctual impulses in motion—their self-preservative instinct, their love of aggression, their need for love, and their impulse to attain pleasure and avoid pain. . . . For sociology, which deals with the behavior of man in society, can be nothing other than applied psychology." (*New Introductory Lectures*, p. 244.)

Thus Freud not only neglected the social situation as a motive for behavior, but stood everything on its head by regarding social situations as the expression of people's ideas or unconscious strivings. From this point of view, war, for example, is the expression of aggressive instincts, and social feeling the expression of latent sexual feeling.

2. As a result of Freud's conviction that outworn, unconscious ideas dominate action, *his scientific method for understanding human behavior is overconcerned with retrospection and rooted in a narrow biologism.* That is, he is much preoccupied with unravelling an individual's past, and in evaluating the strength and interplay of his instinctive biological drives. This retrospective and biological interest is fostered—as we have just seen—at the expense of sociological interest. In actual treatment of an individual case this means intensive biographical investigation and personality probing and dissection with only cursory attention to the problems of conduct and practical life. As a result of this concern with the past and with the world of ideas, psychoanalysis has become too descriptive and abstract: a great deal of space and attention is devoted in its literature to descriptions—often very acute and subtle —of the devious complex ways in which ideas become interrelated or changed by their impact on each other. Much of the fascination of psychoanalysis lies in this skillful pursuit and capture of changing or developing ideas, a pursuit which too often loses its relation to the hard facts of life, and affords a kind of relief to the patient which is not basic and therefore not sustained.

3. Freudianism has a social orientation that is much too narrow. Though it sometimes disclaims any interest in morals or ethics, it has an implicit acceptance of most contemporary middle-class standards. This is revealed in its attitude toward women, in its notion of what is normal, in its standards of success and failure, in its attitude toward social progress, and in its fundamental

Tip Card

Keep in your wallet as a handy reference

Total	15%	20%
$1	.15	.20
$2	.30	.40
$3	.45	.60
$4	.60	.80
$5	.75	1.00
$6	.90	1.20
$7	1.05	1.40
$8	1.20	1.60
$9	1.35	1.80
$10	1.50	2.00
$20	3.00	4.00
$30	4.50	6.00
$40	6.00	8.00
$50	7.50	10.00
$60	9.00	12.00
$70	10.50	14.00
$80	12.00	16.00
$90	13.50	18.00
$100	15.00	20.00
$200	30.00	40.00

AAdvantage

AAdvantage® Dining

Customer Service

Fax-Back Service

Benefit Questions

For 24-hour
Customer Service

800-479-5981

Membership ID Number

Customer Service

Call us 24 hours a day 7 days a week and speak with one of our Customer Service Representatives to:

- Help you locate restaurants in your area.
- Check on your dining activity.
- Review membership guidelines and benefits.

Fax-Back Service

You may locate restaurants by zip code, area code and prefix or four-character location codes. After you've entered the fax number where you want the listings sent, they'll be on their way. It's that easy!

How To Use The Fax-Back Service

1) Call our 24-hour, toll-free number: 1-800-479-5981

2) Follow the prompts that will direct you to our fax-back service.

3) To access a list of participating restaurants, press 1 to search by zip code; press 2 to search by area code and prefix; press 3 to have a list of location codes faxed to you. (Once you've received the location codes, call the 800 number and follow the prompts.)

4) Enter the fax number, including area code, where you wish to have the listing faxed and press the (#) key. The fax number will be repeated back to you for verification. If correct, press the number 1 and hang up. Your fax will be on the way.

5) You will receive a list of all participating establishments from your selection as well as those within the surrounding area. The establishments that are the closest to your selection will appear in bold.

pessimism. It is true that the psychological level of integration has its own independent laws, and justifies a separate scientific discipline, but the psychological level stands in constant and intimate interrelationship to both physiology and sociology, with influences moving back and forth between all levels. Freudianism, which arose as a progressive influence at a time when psychiatry was dominated by the mechanical material interests of the pathological anatomists, *has almost completely lost interest in the material physiological basis of mental function, and has gone over to the other great extreme* of depicting all nervous disorders as psychological problems, and even in regarding many organic diseases as mainly psychological disorders. The current interest in "psychosomatic" medicine is dominated by this Freudian point of view.

In relation to the social advance toward a better life it can therefore be said that the psychoanalytic tradition is characterized by certain evasive or reactionary tendencies. It is fascinated by the past at the expense of the present, and imputes excessive—at times almost magical—powers to the force of analytic insight, at the expense of action. Although the whole range of schools of psychoanalysis recognize to some degree the interdependence of social relationships and ideas, the psychoanalytic tradition always greatly overvalues the primary influence of ideas. To make matters worse it endows ideas with an abstract independent existence, as "instincts," or makes them relatively independent by relating them to experiences long past, or derivative from an abstract cultural tradition. It minimizes the basic fact that ideas are derivative from social relationships, and are continually modified by changing relationships.

As a consequence, psychoanalysis is very attractive to many troubled people who are unable, unwilling, or otherwise unprepared to undertake the action necessary for their social adjustment. It is no accident that psychoanalysis makes a particular point of being independent of ethical considerations and that psychoanalysts are often scornful of the kind of psychiatry that gives advice.

Even the more advanced psychoanalysts leave big loopholes for the orthodox point of view. A crucial point concerns the changeability of human nature. The instinct theory makes human nature relatively fixed. But so does an undue emphasis on childhood experience. This aspect of psychoanalytic theory can be regarded as a scientific expression of the popular notion that the tree's inclined the way the twig is bent (which, by the way, does not accord with the botanical facts). "There is no doubt whatever," wrote Horney (*New Ways in Psychoanalysis*, p. 152), "that childhood experiences exert a decisive influence on development . . . with some persons this development essentially stops at the age of five, with some it stops in adolescence, with others at around thirty, with a few it goes on until old age." One of the more critical analysts, Bernard Robbins, for example, attacks another psychoanalyst, Franz Alexander, for his insistence on the biological origin of certain human attitudes, but in the course of his attack shares the assumption that neuroses are based upon childhood experiences. "The question is clear," he wrote. "What are the conditions in infancy and childhood out of which neuroses evolve?" But cannot adult life induce neuroses? Other analysts discard the instinct theory, but regard the need for sexual gratification as a "basic biological drive," like hunger and thirst, and proceed to exaggerate its social function. This reminds one of the man who was a staunch vegetarian, except for veal cutlets, which he liked.

As scientists and physicians it would be absurd for us to take the view that we are opposed to the analysis of neurotic symptoms. In the plain English meaning of the term analysis we certainly recognize the frequent necessity for the careful, detailed and painstaking unravelling of mental symptoms or personal problems. We must also recognize that free association, slips of tongue, dream analysis, the understanding of symbols and of mental mechanisms are all invaluable aids to such analysis. But we do not regard the analysis as an end in itself. The end point of every analysis of a neurotic symptom should be an understanding of the social relationships that both initiated and maintained the symptoms or disorder, or an understanding of the physiological derangement involved. In a few cases the mere understanding can bring enormous satisfaction and relief, but in most cases the analysis must lead to a line of action that would serve to adjust the social relationships or relieve the physiological derangement. The analysis in other words is a preliminary to treatment and is not in itself a treatment, just as historical analysis is a guide to social action but no substitute for it.

A socially oriented psychiatry built on democratic standards need not limit itself to standards and criteria of a merely upper class psychiatry. It should not, for example, regard comfortable adaptation to a static social order as either a possible or desirable standard or psychotherapeutic goal. If frustration, bitterness, aggressiveness, and depression become the lot of a portion of our population under certain social conditions, we can at least reject the paraphernalia of terminology, mechanisms, apologetics and fatalisms that support the resignation of psychiatry to this kind of discontent. In practice, over and over again, much of our contemporary psychiatry tells the neurotics to seek within themselves the causes of their discontent. It thus cultivates the fiction of the isolated man, of automatic instincts unfolding with an inner energy, and obscures the true picture of man and personality developing within a social context. For this reason a socially oriented psychiatry must erect its own goals and describe its own standards. It must, moreover, shape its own tools to cope with the various kinds of discontent (not always dignified with the term neurosis) found in our society. The solid basis for such an undertaking lies in a broad social orientation. In the face of real problems, a preaching psychiatry that tells its patients to "adapt themselves," or bases its appeal upon encouragement or exhortation is as empty as the appeals for popular morale would be in an unjust war. Likewise, a merely cathartic psychiatry that aims to divert or diffuse disturbing impulses into socially useful or neutral channels, tends to disregard the real origin of neurotic difficulties and the material basis for their transmutation. Lacking a solid basis, its value is bound to peter out as soon as the hard facts of life disturb the individual again. Our psychiatry must pay more than lip service to "social influences," "ego and super-ego problems," and "contributing situational factors." It is always timely for our psychiatrists to reexamine the philosophy underlying their activities, and to restate their basic convictions. To that end the following propositions may form a fruitful basis for discussion:

Renewed emphasis must be placed on the material basis of mind, but mind must not be regarded as a phenomenon that can be studied in isolation, i.e., apart from its anatomical and physiological substrate and its sociological superstructure. We must not accept any picture of mind or consciousness which endows it with fixed or static qualities, for not only can human nature be changed, but it is in fact always in process of change. The nervous system may be regarded as primarily an integrative organ, mediating on the one hand between the other bodily organs and systems, and on the other hand mediating the connections between separate organisms in the social body. Deficiencies and disturbances in these integrative functions sometimes occur, and at times there may be a relative incompleteness of integrative efficiency from brain injury, during coma, delirium, sleep, dreams, intoxication and the like. We need not, however, regard the products of deficient integration as more important, more characteristic or more cogent than the refined products of a more highly integrated function. *In vino veritas*, for example, is an untrue proposition. The partial, distorted and fragmentary revelations of intoxication may be significant and interesting, but the drunken man does not reveal his "true" personality: he merely reveals the kind of personality he has when he is drunk. The same applies to sleep and dreams. The time has come to reassert the importance of conscious activity, in contrast to the enormous emphasis on the obscurities of the remote unconscious that has characterized Freudianism and its offshoots. It is not perhaps widely enough realized to what an extent Freud has belittled the significance of consciousness. The following passage from Freud's *Interpretations of Dreams* (Brill's translation, Macmillan, N. Y., 1933, p. 56) is typical:

"A return from the over-estimation of the property of consciousness is the indispensable preliminary to any genuine insight into the course of psychic events. As Lipps has said, 'the unconscious must be accepted as the general basis of the psychic life.' The unconscious is the larger circle which includes the smaller circle of the conscious, everything conscious has a preliminary unconscious stage, whereas the unconscious can stop at this stage, and yet claim to be considered a full psychic function. The unconscious is the true psychic reality: in its inner nature it is just as imperfectly communicated to us by the data of consciousness as the external world by the reports of our sense organs."

With due regard to the limitations of physical endowment (which are also susceptible to change) it is, in the final analysis, social structure that determines human behavior together with the ideals and ideologies which motivate behavior. Without some form of social organization, personality as we know it would have no meaning or existence. Patterns of behavior, language, ideas and personalities, all owe their being to the social context in which they arise and cannot claim an independent existence. Man has no fixed instincts of social behavior. Not even the pattern of normal sexual activity can be regarded as instinctive and innate: contemporary normal patterns of sexual maturity owe their development to a social context in which the monogamous heterosexual family ideal is dominant. A socially oriented psychiatry need not assume the existence of innate inherent ideas related to social objectives. In this sense it rejects the inheritance of acquired traits, the inheritance of sexual antipathies or ideals, or racial loyalties, of a "collective unconscious," of ancient dream symbols and the like.

Freud's dictum, "Thought is behavior in rehearsal," (*Das Denken ist ein Probehandeln*) should be raised to the dignity of a central idea. All thought is inextricably bound to behavior: changes in behavior—in the relation of one individual to others—effect changes in thought; and conversely, disorders of thought produce disorders of behavior. The key to an understanding of social behavior lies in an understanding of the organization of society—of its productive relationships in general, and the individual working relationships in particular. These economic motivations of behavior however should not be too narrowly regarded: individuals themselves are not always directly motivated by economic needs, for there is a large intervening area of group ideology, surviving tradition and past habit (all in complex interrelationship) lying between the laws of economic necessity and individual behavior in specific situations.

Treatment of individuals should not be limited to talk alone. For one thing, the integrative apparatus, the nervous system, must be kept in good health, since disturbances in thought and behavior are often due to bad health, fatigue, tension and overwork. But for the great majority of people who look to psychiatrists for help it must be said that there can be no real mental health without a healthy harmonious working relationship to other individuals and to society as a whole. Psychiatrists should therefore emphasize the predominant importance of the family and social situation for the child, and of working conditions and social conditions for the adult. We wish to treat our patients in close collaboration with social workers or others whose interest and activity embrace the whole social milieu, and we share with social workers an immediate interest in the alleviation of unemployment, freedom from the threat of war, the provision of adequate food and shelter for all, the maintenance of all our liberties, the improvement of working conditions, the provision of play facilities for children and of sport and cultural activities for adults, in security for the sick and aged, and in improved educational facilities for all.

Certain psychoanalysts will enthusiastically support these objectives, but will add that so far as their patients are concerned we must make the best of society as it is. These "advanced" psychoanalysts picture our society as a fairly uniform culture, and picture the culture as a body of ideas permeating our society. They overlook the fact that a culture is not primarily a system of ideas, but a system of active social and working relationships, and that in our own society the individual has considerable freedom to choose the kind of relationship he wishes to assume toward others. In this sense there is more than one kind of culture in our society toward which the individual can exercise his freedom of choice. Personality problems which are engendered by experiences, social relationships and situations, are supported and changed by experiences, situations and social relationships too. Those "advanced" psychoanalysts who acquire this insight are being forced step by step to deny the very premises upon which much of their professional activity depends. For if action and social relationships, work and working relationships are the key to any fundamental therapy of personality disorders, obviously the psychoanalytic procedure is then no longer therapy, but rather a preliminary to therapy: psychotherapy then becomes indistinguishable from elucidation or education, and these seldom require private tutoring arrangements. Common sense considerations, sound ethical values, good work for worthy ends, close identification with the popular forces of our democracy and constant exposure to their wholesome influence become basic. And insofar as mental disturbances are related to physiological disorders, psychoanalysis in the strict sense of the term tends to become less important too.

The trouble is that most psychoanalysts find themselves deeply committed to certain psychoanalytic procedures, make their living from them, have developed certain organizational and institutional ties and have too often tended to isolate themselves from medical practice on the one hand and from popular movements on the other. A practicing psychoanalyst usually sees private patients with neurotic problems in isolation in his home, hotel or office, for one hour sessions, usually several times a week and over a period of months or years. It is mainly middle class and white collar elements who are attracted to psychoanalysts for help, and it is mainly these who can afford this type of treatment. Industrial workers are a distinct rarity in psychoanalytic practice. This unsatisfactory state of affairs has stimulated interest in a number of new developments in psychoanalytic circles: a closer interest in medicine (though in psychosomatic medicine the psychoanalysts meet medicine on their own terms), experimentation with more rapid forms of treatment (brief psychoanalysis) and group therapy. It is significant that under wartime conditions almost all practicing psychoanalysts who became Army or Navy psychiatrists soon devised or accepted new, quick techniques for the treatment of nervous disorders. The emerging demands of industrial psychiatry will require similar adjustments. But each new progressive advance involves either a dilution or contradiction of some Freudian principle. Psychoanalytic theory, like many other things, has been exposed to many changes since the war. The psychoanalyst who accepts group therapy as a valuable new technique, for example, exposes himself at the same time to some refreshing influences emanating from the people. The analyst soon realizes that group therapy can be most effective if combined with cooperative working relationships for useful ends and operated as a joint democratic enterprise. But this is no longer psychoanalysis but the good life itself.

Neurotic complaints revolve about internal conflicts. Freud believed the conflict is precipitated by the opposition between instinctive drives and the repressive demands of organized society. To Horney the conflict represented a clash between the demands of the present and the attitudes created by one's past. In reality neurotic conflicts are both engendered and maintained by the contradictory nature of the actual social relationships in which we are involved; they can be regarded as mental reflections of real relationships. The mental conflicts cannot be resolved until there is a corresponding resolution of these contradictory relationships. There is a time-lag involved in the change, to be sure, but it is not as great as some psychoanalysts suppose.

A single brief case history can illustrate our point of view: *Lady in the Dark*. In this motion picture we were presented with an especially seductive psychoanalytic formulation and solution of a woman's problem—in technicolor. The heroine is a business executive who is depicted as unhappy (*i.e.*, neurotic) because of the conflict between her unconscious wish to be a woman (*i.e.*, passive) and to be successful in her career (*i.e.*, to be masculine or active). She has repressed her innate femininity because of a childhood experience (scolded by her father for trying to be pretty like her mother). This early experience is recalled to her by psychoanalysis; the picture ends when the lady—who is now supposed to be no longer in the dark—capitulates to her femininity and yields herself and her position to an aggressive man.

Actually the lady's conflict did not lie in the past, but in the present: the conflict between business success and femininity is a real conflict created by the position of women in our society. This conflict is not resolved by submission to the orthodox pattern of femininity, and such submission should not be represented as an acquiescence to an overwhelming innate need. The psychoanalytic formulation of the film represents nothing but misstatement and gross evasion of a real and typical woman's problem, the solution of which lies very much in the realm of practical affairs.

But this is only one particular type of problem, and there are many others. A consideration of social relationships is basic to an understanding of most of them, but it would be naive and mechanical to overlook the intricacies involved in this dependency. Although adult personality patterns are not rigidly fixed, it must be recognized that mature individuals have acquired a personality of their own, related to biological endowment, past experiences, ideological influences, varying individual and social pressures, long-range individual and group needs, and condition of health, in addition to their immediate social situation. Moreover, their personality makes them react to their social situation in many complex and often contrary and bewildering ways. It is the main task of analysis to reveal these influences and to relieve the bewilderment that is characteristic of the neurotic development, so that effective action can follow. The complexity of the processes involved is, however, too often exaggerated. Most people are going to get relief from their unhappy conflicts by a change in their social relationships and social functions; even the analyzed patients will not escape the necessity of maintaining wholesome social relationships too. The transition to wholesomeness may be rather difficult for some people, and practically impossible for a few, unless there are strong incentives for doctor or patient or both to expend the time, care and patience required for the change.

These broad considerations are intended to apply to the generality of people, and not to the exceptional few. The great prevalence of anxiety emphasized by one contemporary psychoanalytic school is surely the reflection of the sense of insecurity that isolated individuals must feel in a society that is at times too harshly competitive. The correct antidote is a consolidation of social feeling with those broad sections of our population that have the need for real social solidarity. The mere activity of participation in cooperative work for socially useful ends is therapeutic. It creates moreover the preconditions for a successful advance of our democracy to larger social objectives. It is only the realization of these social objectives that can secure full happiness and mental health to our people. Psychoanalysis after a long and devious detour will sooner or later have to base itself on these fundamentals which it sought for a while to evade. Meanwhile the fuller elaboration of a truly scientific psychology remains an important present task.

Envoi, 1984

When this sketch of a very famous man was published thirty years ago, it yielded a few compliments but otherwise attracted surprisingly little interest. Meerloo, a psychoanalyst, reviewed it for The New York Times *and said it was "fascinating... reads like a novel." The* New Republic *called it "intriguing," and Waldo Frank in* The Nation *said, "A vivid magnificent old man emerges." But for the most part the media gave it scant attention, and the few other reviews that appeared were tepid and unenthusiastic, if not hostile. The* New Yorker *did not review it but published instead a parody by Wolcott Gibbs entitled "A Couch of My Own," which relied on the absurdity of having the little man on the couch analyzing the great analyst, while the simplicity of my prose was reduced to a kindergarten level. Edward Bernays, a prominent New York public relations consultant and a nephew of Freud's, complained to the publisher that this was a one-sided account written by a brash young man in a spirit of antagonism and resistance, and questioned both its ethics and veracity, while at the same time asserting that the book revealed Freud as wise and profound. I think that many did not know what to make of an approach to Freud that was anything less than adulatory. Sales were disappointing and the publisher soon withdrew it.*

But the book hung in. A small book club issued it as a selection; after a lapse of years a new edition was brought out by Bobbs-Merrill, and then came a series of translations into Spanish, French, Italian and Swedish. McGraw-Hill later republished it, and the present is thus its fifth English edition. The book is now well known to Freud's biographers and commentators, and seems to have become one of the incunabula of the movement. Ironically, I may be best remembered as

The Man Who Was Analyzed by Freud.

What has happened to Freudianism since the book first appeared? It is hard to say what authentic psychoanalysis is these days, because the term is self-applied to so many offshoots and divisions, as their numbers continue to multiply by fission. To a degree the size and impact of the psychoanalytic movement can be gauged by the number of psychoanalysts. In 1950 the Roster *of the International Psycho-analytic Association, which traces its lineage to Sigmund Freud, listed worldwide about a thousand analysts, by reason of their membership in an accredited national psychoanalytic association. About half of them were in the United States. In the 1982* Roster *there are over 5000 listed, one third of whom, roughly 1800, are in the United States. In the corresponding period the membership of the American Psychiatric Association rose from 5,800 in 1950 to nearly 28,000 in 1983. The psychoanalysts can be found mostly in the urban centers of both coasts, in Chicago, and a few big cities, with almost none in rural America. Unlike many other national organizations, the American Psychoanalytic Association requires its members to be physicians, though there are countless psychologists, social workers, nonaccred-ited physicians and others who call themselves analysts. The Argen-tine (population 28,000,000) has 286 psychoanalysts, Israel (pop. 4,000,000) 50, Japan (pop. 118,000,000) 23, United Kingdom (pop. 56,000,000) 350, with almost all in London, and India (pop. 670,000,000) 36, of whom only ten have a doctor's degree. The Soviet Union once had a psychoanalytic association, but no longer, nor do any of the other socialist countries. It would seem there are really not many accredited psychoanalysts in the world, that these are largely concentrated in a few big cities of the industrialized West, especially in the United States, and many are not physicians. The significance of these numbers must be evaluated cautiously since they are much influenced by both eligibility requirements and economic factors.*

Psychoanalysis is time-consuming and expensive; as its economic base has always been private practice, it cannot survive among the poor or in poor countries and is sensitive to periods of economic reces-sion. Moreover, it does not lend itself to large public health enterprises or national health systems. When the National Health Service was in-troduced in Britain, psychoanalytic activity immediately declined, and is now seldom encountered outside of London. In the United States, cults and competing therapies crowd the field, and the new physiologic treatment methods prevail in the major psychoses. In the past few decades while medical literature has burgeoned, psychoanalytic interests have declined. In 1950 there were 87 items listed in the comprehensive Index Medicus under the subject heading Psychoanalysis—in 1982 there were 47. Though much diminished in importance, psychoanalysis still exerts a strong influence not only on psychiatry, but especially among our educated middle classes, among the literati, and in the arts: perhaps that is where its strongest adherents can be found today. It is also the middle classes that feed the clientele into the offices of the private practicing analysts.

In scientific circles psychoanalysis has not fared well. Piaget, our leading developmental psychologist, paid very little attention to Freud, and wrote, "his theoretical conceptions now require a general overhaul." The late Schneirla, our chief authority on instinct, ignored him. In the huge six-volume collaborative compendium on Psychology edited by Koch 25 years ago, Freud is hardly mentioned in half the volumes, and gets a mixed reception in the rest. Psychoanalytic influence on anthropology and sociology has been transient and very limited. The main trouble has been that psychoanalysis never developed a serious research tradition. In one of his earliest papers on hysteria, Freud himself apologized for his abandonment of the method and even the language of science. "I find it strange," he said, "to be writing case histories that read like novels, and which lack, so to speak, any scientific features." Arnold Cooper, in his presidential address before the American Psychoanalytic Association in 1982 said, "At the present time the scarcity of psychoanalytic researchers seriously threatens our continued psychoanalytic development. Our exciting debates will become arid if they are not sprinkled with new data. . . . Even if we do not feel impelled by our scientific and theoretical curiosity, we might respond to the demands of a society that will not forever allow us to practice clinical psychoanalysis without evidence of its efficacy." The Nobel prize winner biologist Medawar recently complained more bluntly that psychoanalysis "will remain one of the saddest and strangest of all landmarks in the history of twentieth-century thought." (Plato's Republic, 1982)

Special scientific attention has recently been focused on the therapeutic value of psychoanalysis. Remarkably little interest or study has been directed to this theme, though the British Medical Associa-

207

tion over half a century ago called for systematic testing of its claims. Yet all the evidence to date on psychoanalysis and other psychotherapeutic modalities adds up to hardly more than the simple declaration that talking often helps. In a scholarly commentary on the available literature, Garfield concluded, "We have a long way to go before we can speak authoritatively about the efficacy, generality, or specificity of psychotherapy. Until we are able to secure more definitive research data, the efficacy of psychotherapy will remain a controversial issue." (Biol. Psychiat., 18:1104, 1983)

In the broad area of psychiatric theory the discussions will go on, but the terms of the discussions are changing: proof is now demanded, and authoritative pronouncements dressed in rhetoric are rejected. For a long time the common response of psychoanalysis to its critics was to call attention to their subjective failings or ignorance. But the Aristotelian fallacy of argumentum ad hominem can no longer be employed. ("If you have no case, attack the plaintiff!") That weapon was used too much against Freud himself. The Viennese public, never friendly to Freud, would gossip in the coffee-houses about his arrogance: "Zuerst Freud und dann allmächtiger Gott—first Freud and then God Almighty," but Freud quite properly told me, "People should interest themselves in psychoanalysis, and not in my person." (p. 121) Unfortunately, however, he made ample use of this tactic in refuting his opponents. It cannot be denied that the subjective element is present in scientific work, creating bias and distortion, but the proper corrective is the scientific method, which requires data and evidence to yield the truth. If one protests that the material does not lend itself to scientific validation, then one should abandon the pretense that it is a science.

Actually, Freud made rather modest claims for the therapeutic efficacy of psychoanalysis, recognizing that it was of little value in the major psychoses (where he thought biochemistry would provide the answers), and thought it best suited to the milder neuroses or character disorders where unconscious factors play a role. "The future," wrote Freud, "will probably attribute far greater importance to psychoanalysis as the science of the unconscious than as a therapeutic procedure." (Britannica, 14th ed.) He did believe that his disclosure of the unconscious heralded a new epoch in human history, comparable to the discoveries of Copernicus and Darwin. My own anticipation is that future generations (if we survive) will be especially interested in *studying how psychoanalysis became a unique product of our culture, and how in turn it influenced that culture.*

Joseph Wortis

INDEX